Voter Registration Application

Before completing this form, review the General, Application, and State specific instructions.

| Are you a citizen of the United States of America? | ☐ Yes | ☐ No | This space for office use only |
| Will you be 18 years old on or before election day? | ☐ Yes | ☐ No | |

If you checked "No" in response to either of these questions, do not complete form.
(Please see state-specific instructions for rules regarding eligibility to register prior to age 18.)

D0902156

1	(Circle one) Mr. Mrs. Miss Ms.	Last Name	First Name	Midd...
2	Home Address		Apt. or Lot #	City/Town
3	Address Where You Get Your Mail If Different From Above		City/Town	State	Zip Code

| **4** | Date of Birth ___ / ___ / ___
Month Day Year | **5** | Telephone Number (optional) | **6** | ID Number - (See Item 6 in the instructions for your state) |
| **7** | Choice of Party
(see item 7 in the instructions for your State) | **8** | Race or Ethnic Group
(see item 8 in the instructions for your State) | | |

9 I have reviewed my state's instructions and I swear/affirm that:
- I am a United States citizen
- I meet the eligibility requirements of my state and subscribe to any oath required.
- The information I have provided is true to the best of my knowledge under penalty of perjury. If I have provided false information, I may be fined, imprisoned, or (if not a U.S. citizen) deported from or refused entry to the United States.

Please sign full name (or put mark) ▲

Date: ___ / ___ / ___
Month Day Year

If you are registering to vote for the first time: please refer to the application instructions for information on submitting copies of valid identification documents with this form.

Please fill out the sections below if they apply to you.

If this application is for a **change of name,** what was your name before you changed it?

| **A** | Mr.
Mrs.
Miss
Ms. | Last Name | First Name | Middle Name(s) | (Circle one)
Jr Sr II III IV |

If you were **registered before but this is the first time you are registering from the address in Box 2**, what was your address where you were registered before?

| **B** | Street (or route and box number) | Apt. or Lot # | City/Town/County | State | Zip Code |

If you live in a rural area but do not have a street number, or if you have no address, please show on the map where you live.

C
- Write in the names of the crossroads (or streets) nearest to where you live.
- Draw an **X** to show where you live.
- Use a dot to show any schools, churches, stores, or other landmarks near where you live, and write the name of the landmark.

NORTH ▲

Example

Route #2

● Grocery Store

Woodchuck Road

Public School ●   X

If the applicant is unable to sign, who helped the applicant fill out this application? Give name, address and phone number (phone number optional).

D

Mail this application to the address provided for your State.

Revised 10/29/2008

MyPolitics

The 2008 Presidential Campaign Workbook

TONY ROBINSON

PEARSON
Longman

New York San Francisco Boston
London Toronto Sydney Tokyo Singapore Madrid
Mexico City Munich Paris Cape Town Hong Kong Montreal

Editor in Chief: Eric Stano
Executive Marketing Manager: Ann Stypuloski
Media Supplements Editor: Brian Belardi
Production Coordinator: Scarlett Lindsay
Cover Designer/Manager: Nancy Danahy
Cover Images: Men and woman running: © Anthony Marsland, Stone+/Getty
    Images; White House: © Hisham Ibrahim, Stockbyte/Getty Images; Running
    Track: © James Oliver, Digital Vision/Getty Images; Stars: © PhotDisc/
    Getty Images
Cover Montage: Nancy Danahy
Senior Manufacturing Buyer: Alfred C. Dorsey
Printer and Binder: Courier Corporation / Stoughton
Cover Printer: Courier Corporation / Stoughton

Please visit us at www.ablongman.com

ISBN-13: 978-0-205-63939-7
ISBN-10:   0-205-63939-9

2 3 4 5 6 7 8 9 10—CRS—11 10 09 08

CONTENTS

How did the Republican and Democratic nominees inspire their troops at the Party Conventions? Hear for yourself in exercises one and two.

What was "Ford's infamous gaffe," and how did a journalist's question devastate candidate Dukakis in 1988? Watch for yourself in exercise eight.

Have you heard of the Daisy Girl ad? Reagan and the Bear? The Swift Boat ads? View them all in exercise four.

What are the top zip codes and industries that give to Democrats? Who gives to the Republicans? To find out, turn to exercise thirteen.

Is the media obsessed with the political horse race and negative scandals? To investigate, go to exercise nine.

Will there be a popular mandate in 2008? Who will vote, and for what? Learn the answers in exercises eleven and fourteen.

A presidential election opens up fascinating questions about the values of the American people, the nature of American democracy, and the meaning of American history—and you will explore many of those questions in the interactive exercises in this book. Organized around an exploration of 2008 election events as they unfold, the exercises in this book stand on their own as a unique, hands-on exploration in American democracy. They can also serve as a supplement to standard textbooks in American politics, allowing students to test theories against reality, to explore and create political knowledge on their own, and to enjoy classic and current moments in American political history. Elections are dynamic and engaging political events; with the innovative political "labs" in this book, you can be similarly dynamic and engaged as you follow them.

I would like to thank those who played an important role in helping me to complete this book. My editor at Pearson Longman, Eric Stano, deserves credit for the original vision behind this book, and played a key role at every stage in seeing the project through to completion. Other editorial staff at Pearson Longman, especially Donna Garnier, helped ensure a professional product. The project would not have got off the ground without the initial creative efforts of Professor Julie Dolan, from Macalester College. My research assistant at the University of Colorado–Denver, Stephen Noriega, came through with all sorts of details, including talking through exercise ideas, chasing down permissions, and helping with software glitches. I extend a heartfelt thanks to all my college elections classes over the years, where many of these exercise ideas incubated. Most of all, my warmest thoughts go out to my wife, my teenage daughter, and my newborn girl: Minsun, Donalyn, and Sora, thank you so much for all the time, love, and support you have given.

Congratulations! You are about to become a creative scholar of "the most important election in history." How can that be?

It's long been said that the two most important presidential elections in history are always the same two elections: the current election and the next one. This tongue-in-cheek statement expresses an important truth—every presidential election captures the imagination and energy of the nation, involves fundamental choices about the direction of the country, and lays the foundation for the next clash for the presidency, four years down the road. When you first open this book, America will be in the heat of the current election; by the time you finish, the country will be facing the next one. As a student of election 2008, you will have an up-close view of some of the most exciting events in American politics—events that offer a unique opportunity for memorable study and learning.

It is the goal of this book's collection of interactive exercises (you could call them political science "labs") to guide you in engaging election 2008, to open up an exciting world of firsthand political research, and to help make election 2008 your most *personally* memorable election—whether it is truly "the most important election" in history or not.

This is no textbook. We all know that sometimes textbooks can be dry and even boring, and that it's not always easy to learn and remember the lessons encountered in chapter after chapter of passive reading. As a supplement to the typical textbook, this book takes a different approach. Here, you will learn about politics through hands-on interactive exercises, viewing video clips, visiting unique Web sites, and opening powerful databases. Though standard textbooks and traditional methods of study are vital, *students often learn best by doing*—by actively engaging in course materials, by interacting with various datasets, and by experiencing information in multiple mediums. That's what this book is all about.

Through interactive exercises, this book guides you in locating and utilizing some of the best political resources on the Web. The exercises parallel the unfolding presidential election of 2008, allowing you to learn about events as they happen. As you watch current campaign ads, for example, this workbook will guide you to places where you can view classic ads through history. You may have heard about the "Daisy Girl" ad, or Reagan's famous "Morning in America" ad. Through this workbook, you will view them for yourself. You will also build your own campaign ad from stock Internet footage, narration, and music, and will master the information needed to evaluate the current set of campaign ads.

In another exercise, as you prepare to view the 2008 presidential debates, you will view dramatic moments from past presidential debates. You will learn why political scholars everywhere remember Reagan's phrase "there you go again," as well another famous quip: "You're no Jack Kennedy." You will see John F. Kennedy himself, in a classic debate against Richard Nixon. From these historic clips, you will learn what to look for in the current debates, which you can evaluate with the help of an included "debate scorecard." Other exercises will help you to map Electoral College predictions, to predict congressional "swing-seats," to track campaign finances, to evaluate media coverage, and more.

The exercises are fun, but serious, political lessons. Highlights include:

- Each exercise is introduced by a two-page theoretical overview.

- The exercises are presented in step-by-step fashion, guiding you with Internet links to some of the best resources on the Web and advice on how to use the wealth of information at each site.

- Frequent screenshots of what you will be seeing are provided, so that you can always be confident that you are at the right place.

- Each exercise is followed by an attached worksheet, on which you can report your findings as you move through the exercise.

Throughout these exercises, you will be learning a bit of what it means to be a political scientist—exploring databases, evaluating political events as they unfold, comparing today's events to classic episodes in history. When done, you will have encountered, evaluated, and produced substantial first hand knowledge about American elections. You will have mastered the events of election 2008—everything from which campaign ads were most effective to what the people were saying with their votes. You will have experienced an election you won't soon forget.

To help you make the most of this workbook, here are some tips:

- The exercises are built around Internet resources. Though the websites in this book are generally stable and predictable, there is always the chance that some links become broken, some websites will change, etc. All such changes will be monitored by the author of this book, and updates and corrections to every exercise will be posted regularly at www.pearson.com/mypolitics. **Before you begin any exercise, you should go to www.pearson.com/mypolitics, and note any updates or corrections related to it.**

- Each exercise is followed by a worksheet. As you move through the exercise, you will be instructed at various points to fill in your answers and thoughts on the worksheet. It is best to detach the worksheet before you begin the exercise and to fill it in step-by-step as you move through the exercise itself.

- As you move through each exercise, you will note that links you are to follow or places you are to click on a webpage are always printed in **bold font.** Whenever you see **bold font,** you should note that you are being asked to perform an action on a webpage.

- When you are instructed to fill in your worksheet, the directions are *printed in italics.* Whenever you see *italicized font,* you should note that you are being asked to complete a step in the worksheet.

- At www.pearson.com/mypolitics, you can find downloadable versions of all worksheets. These downloadable worksheets will allow you to type your information into the worksheet on your computer, and expand your ideas as much as desired, without being bound to the space limitations of hardcopy worksheets in this book.

- Throughout the exercises, you will type various Web addresses into your browser. It is easy to make mistakes in typing addresses—so whenever a page doesn't load correctly, you should double-check to be sure you typed the address correctly. Please note that most addresses begin with "**www**," in which case you needn't type "**http://**" before the address itself. Whenever an address *doesn't* begin with "www," the exercise will note the full address (such as http://livingroomcandidate.movingimage.us). In such cases, you *will* need to type "**http://**" before the rest of the address.

- Following the exercises, there is a section of reflection questions to guide further thinking on the subject. Your instructor might use these questions to stimulate classroom discussion on the themes in these exercises.

**Enough preliminaries;
turn to page 1 to move on to election 2008!**

This book is meant to supplement your teaching in American Politics and Elections courses. It provides a set of hands-on political science "labs," built around the unfolding events of the 2008 presidential election. The exercises build on my own insights as a longtime teacher of elections, and the recent success I have found in utilizing rapidly exploding Internet resources to study events as they unfold in real time.

Though elections are naturally exciting and are terrific teaching opportunities, instructors know that any subject can be more enlivened with hands-on opportunities for students, multimedia instructional aides, and opportunities for independent student discovery. It's no surprise that students often learn best by doing—by active engagement in exploring, evaluating, and creating political knowledge. We also know that the Web can be a great resource in facilitating this independent exploration—but that it is also a crowded, chaotic, and noisy place, full of junk as well as jewels. It is sometimes hard to know where to direct students for the best and most reliable research. This book helps teachers cut through the clutter of the Web and catalyzes student learning by guiding them through active exploration of high-quality Internet resources.

The workbook is organized into fourteen exercises, each built around an issue that parallels the unfolding election. If completed on a weekly basis throughout the fall term, the exercises are generally organized to parallel the election calendar (i.e., early exercises build on the fall conventions, the debate exercise appears about the same time as the actual presidential debates should be occurring, post-election analysis exercises appear at the end). Still, different college schedules and teaching needs mean that instructors may want to move the exercises around a bit and skip some altogether. There will be no problem in assigning exercises in whatever order desired—the few times when one exercise refers to the findings of another are non-consequential to students completing the assignment.

Each exercise should take students 1.5 to 2 hours to complete. A lot depends on how interested students become in exploring the rich website material they will encounter beyond what is necessary to complete the exercise. Each exercise provides a concise theoretical framing of each issue, helping students to connect the practical exercises with deeper meanings.

It is unavoidable that students may encounter broken links or a few changed Web sites as they work through these exercises. The author will constantly monitor exercises for such problems and updates; corrections and solutions will be posted at www.pearson.com/ mypolitics. Before students begin each exercise, they should go to this site and click the button for the relevant exercise for all such information.

There are many ways to use the exercises in this book. Ideas include:

- A ready-made set of hands-on, out-of-classroom assignments, to supplement regular classroom and textbook learning.

- Enhanced classroom discussions as students come with their own findings and insights based on their learning in these labs. Discussion questions at the end of the workbook can also help stimulate discussion.

- Students can build on what they learn to produce research projects of their own, using the Web resources they have encountered here.

- The text will help students to become "amateur" political scientists, drawing on some of the same data and resources that scholars use in their research. Students will be introduced to some of the basics of producing and evaluating political knowledge on their own.

- Introducing the instructor to a wealth of quality Internet resources and strategies for teaching American politics more effectively.

The 2008 Presidential Campaign Workbook

ISSUE ONE
DEFINING THE DEMOCRATS

Back in the 1980s, two great party leaders offered profoundly different visions of how to address the challenges of America. The Democratic Governor of New York, Mario Cuomo, spoke to the Democratic National Convention of 1984 and urged his party to stand in the tradition of using government help the unfortunate, the old, the young and the less powerful. President Reagan, on the other hand, used his Inaugural address to criticize a government that taxed too heavily, celebrate the individualist spirit, and urge that taxes should not be used to penalize one group of people and lift up another. The following quotes of these leaders reveal the stakes in choosing one party over the other to lead the nation.

> The difference between Democrats and Republicans has always been measured in courage and confidence. The Republicans believe that the wagon train will not make it to the frontier unless some of the old, some of the young, some of the weak are left behind by the side of the trail. 'The strong'—'The strong,' they tell us, 'will inherit the land.' We Democrats believe in something else. We Democrats believe that we can make it all the way with the whole family intact, and we have more than once. Ever since Franklin Roosevelt lifted himself from his wheelchair to lift this nation from its knees — wagon train after wagon train — to new frontiers of education, housing, peace; the whole family aboard, constantly reaching out to extend and enlarge that family; lifting them up into the wagon on the way; blacks and Hispanics, and people of every ethnic group, and native Americans — all those struggling to build their families and claim some small share of America.
>
> — *Mario Cuomo (Governor, NY)*

Those who do work are denied a fair return for their labor by a tax system which penalizes successful achievement and keeps us from maintaining full productivity...In this present crisis, government is not the solution to our problem; government is the problem...We've been tempted to believe that society has become too complex to be managed by self-rule, that government by an elite group is superior to government for, by, and of the people. Well, if no one among us is capable of governing himself, then who among us has the capacity to govern someone else? All of us together, in and out of government, must bear the burden. The solutions we seek must be equitable, with no one group singled out to pay a higher price.

— President Ronald Reagan

As these quotes show, elections matter. Presidential elections are national turning points when voters choose between opposing philosophies of government, competing policies to deal with current challenges, and even between different theories of justice itself, as expressed by the two major parties. In this exercise, you will begin your investigation of differing party philosophies and policy goals by focusing on the Democratic Party. Exercise two, which follows, will focus on the Republican Party. These exercises will help you come to some conclusions about:

- the kind of demographic groups (that is, the kinds of people) that the Democratic and Republican parties target as likely supporters;

- the core issues and philosophy that the different *Parties* stand for;

- the core issues and philosophy that the different presidential *candidates* stand for; and

- strategic considerations that the Democrats and Republicans must weigh as they offer their values and candidates to the voters.

DEFINING THE DEMOCRATS

1. You will begin with an investigation of the kinds of people the Democrats target as likely supporters. Go to **www.democrats.org**. You are now at one of the key homepages of the Democratic Party.

2. One of the key links on the page is called **"People"** (on the menu at the top of the page) If you put your cursor on this link, a list of different voter groups appears that the Democrats are especially reaching out to (see screenshot below).

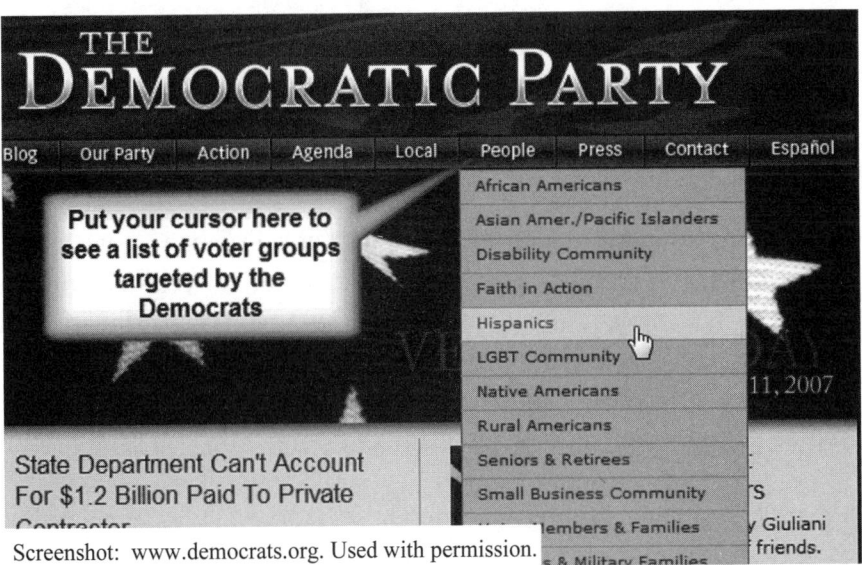

Screenshot: www.democrats.org. Used with permission.

3. Look over this list to get a sense of how the Democrats define the key voters they need to reach out to. *Based on this review, come up with one of these voter groups that is most interesting or surprising to you. On the attached worksheet, list that voter group and include a few sentences of analysis as to why it interests you that the Democrats are targeting this specific group.*

4. Now use your cursor to click on one of the voter groups. It can be the same group that you listed above, or a different one. When you click on the voter group, you are taken to the section of the website where the Democrats present information about why their party, rather than

the Republican Party, is the best to represent this group. The screenshot below focuses on the "Seniors and Retirees" voter group.

Screenshot: www.democrats.org. Used with permission.

★ SENIORS & RETIREES

Another Week, Another Chance for the Republican Presidential Field to Duck Hard Questions

Tonight, the AARP will be hosting a forum for the Republican candidates in Iowa to address issues important to America's seniors but only one of the Republican frontrunners will attend as the others cited "scheduling conflicts."

Read More · Link to this article · Send to a Friend

GET INVOLVED   **SENIORS & RETIREES COMMUNITY HEADLINES**

5. Once you have pulled up your chosen voter group, you will see that the webpage offers a headline on an article of interest to seniors and retirees, has a "get involved" section to the left of the page that informs visitors of different ways to work with the Democratic Party on senior citizen issues, and offers a long list of news articles at the bottom of the page on why the Democrats are strong on senior issues.

6. Explore the voter group page you chose, reading at least one article or following at least one "get involved" link. *Based on what you learn, fill out the worksheet with your conclusion about how the Democratic Party is trying to reach out to and persuade this voter group.*

7. Now you will move on to investigating the kinds of core issues and philosophies that the Democratic Party is offering to the nation. Return to the Democrats' homepage at **www.democrats.org**.

8. Move your cursor to the **"Our Party"** section of the menu. A dropdown list of options appears to help you learn more about the Democrats. Select **"What We Stand For,"** as in the screenshot below.

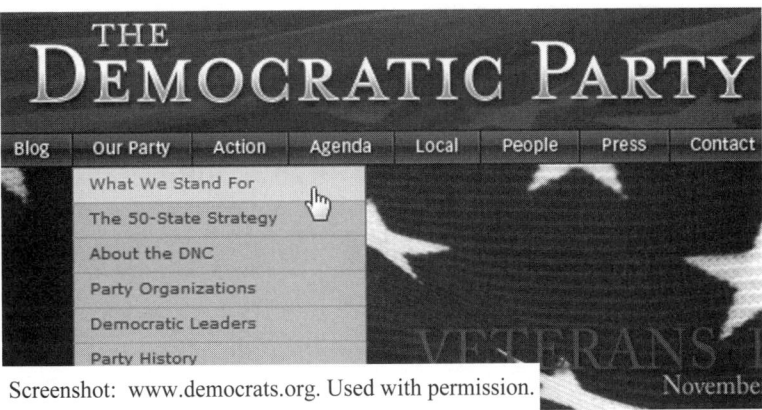

Screenshot: www.democrats.org. Used with permission.

9. You are taken to a section with details of the Democrats' philosophies and policy goals. A **"Guiding Principles"** section includes a section on **"Our Plan."** Click to **"Learn more"** about the Democrats' plan.

Screenshot: www.democrats.org. Used with permission.

What We Stand For

The Democratic Vision

The Democratic Party is committed to keeping our nation safe and expanding opportunity for every American. That commitment is reflected in an agenda that emphasizes the security of our nation, strong economic growth, affordable health care for all Am...............ity, honest govern......

Click here for more details on the Democrats' plan

Guiding Principles

Our Plan
We have a bold new direction for a secure America. We seek: 1) Honest Leadership & Open Government, 2) Real Security, 3) Energy Independence, 4) Economic Prosperity & Educational Excellence, 5) A Healthcare System that Works for Everyone, and 6) Retirement Security. Learn more.

10. You are taken to a six-point Democratic agenda, with four additional "Continued Commitments" at the bottom of the page. Choose *one* issue to learn more about. Click on any *one* of these six points, or on *one* of the four "continued commitments." You will be taken to a brief summary of the Democratic position on this issue. There are also many

additional links to news articles on the subject, but you needn't worry about reading all of these. Just explore the issue a bit so that you get a general sense of the Democratic perspective on this issue.

THE 110TH CONGRESS AND THE DEMOCRATIC AGENDA

The Democratic Agenda: What We Have Accomplished

In 2006, the Democratic Party promised to address six important issues in Congress. Now that Democrats are back in charge in the U.S. House and Senate, you can keep up with the Democrats as they follow through on their promise for a new direction.

① **HONEST LEADERSHIP & OPEN GOVERNMENT**

② **REAL SECURITY**

③ **ENERGY INDEPENDENCE**

④ **ECONOMIC PROSPERITY & EDUCATIONAL EXCELLENCE**

⑤ **A HEALTHCARE SYSTEM THAT WORKS FOR EVERYONE**

⑥ **RETIREMENT SECURITY**

★ what we've done ★ go to the legislation page ★

CONTINUED Commitments

Environment   Civil Rights   Vets/Military   Election Reform

Screenshot: www.democrats.org. Used with permission.

11. *Based on what you learn there, go to the worksheet and include a short description of the Democratic position on the issue you chose.*

12. For additional detail on the underlying philosophy of the Democratic Party, you can explore a bit of the party platform. Repeat step 8-9 above, to return to the **"What We Stand For"** section.

13. Under the **"Guiding Principals"** section on this page there are several links. Click the link for **"Party Platform."**

14. You will be taken to a page with questions and answers about the role of the Party platform and the process of creating it. There is also a link

to the Democrats' **2008 Party Platform. Click that link,** as in the screenshot below.

Screenshot: www.democrats.org. Used with permission.

15. The platform is a thick document, and you won't be reading all of it. But since the platform represents fundamental party values, you can learn a good deal about Democratic thinking by perusing some of it. When the platform has opened, you will find a table of contents, breaking the platform down into several themes (such as "A Strong, Respected America," "Strong, Healthy Families," etc.). Decide which of these themes most interest you (military and defense issues? Issues of Faith and Family?). Go to the section that deals with your issue.

16. Read the section of the platform on the issue that interests you. *Summarize Democratic thinking on this issue on the worksheet.*

17. Now you can investigate how the current Democratic candidate for President thinks about the issues facing America. Go to **www.demconvention.com.** This is one of the homepages where the Democrats provide information about their 2008 Denver Convention. On this page, you will find a link to **"video,"** on the left hand side.

18. Click this link to go to videos of past convention speeches and speeches from the 2008 Democratic Convention (see screenshot on next page).

Screenshot: www.demconvention.com

19. As you can see, you can view all sorts of videos of past Democratic conventions, if you are a political junkie. But for this assignment, all you have to do is click on the links for the 2008 convention. **Choose the link for the last day of the convention,** when the candidate gave his or her nomination acceptance speech.

20. A video of the speech will appear, as in the screenshot on the next page, which is from the 2004 Convention. You do not need to watch the entire speech, but you might enjoy watching some of the campaign hoopla from before or after the speech, just to get a sense of how energetic people at the convention are about their candidate. You should watch about 10 minutes of the candidate's speech (you can pull the video forward or backward to watch the parts you are interested in). As you watch, think about what you learn from the candidate in terms of the core values he or she is standing for as a representative of the Democratic Party.

2004 Convention: Day 4, Part 2

Digg this

Screenshot: www.democrats.org. Used with permission.

21. Watch about ten minutes of the keynote speech by the Democratic nominee. *Based on what you viewed, use your worksheet to summarize a key issue or philosophy that this candidate is offering to the American people.*

22. Finally, you will now investigate some of the strategic considerations that the Democrats must consider as they offer their ideas to the voters.

23. Go to **www.cnn.com/video/.** You are now at the video archive section of CNN news.

24. Toward the bottom of the page, you can search videos by category. Scroll down to the bottom of the page and click the button to search videos **"By Section"** (see screenshot below).

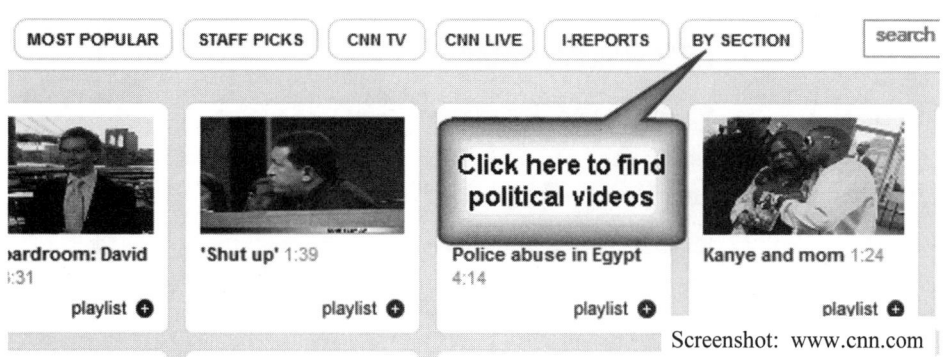

Screenshot: www.cnn.com

25. A menu of CNN video sections appears to the left of the video thumbnails. Click on the **"Politics"** section, as in the screenshot below.

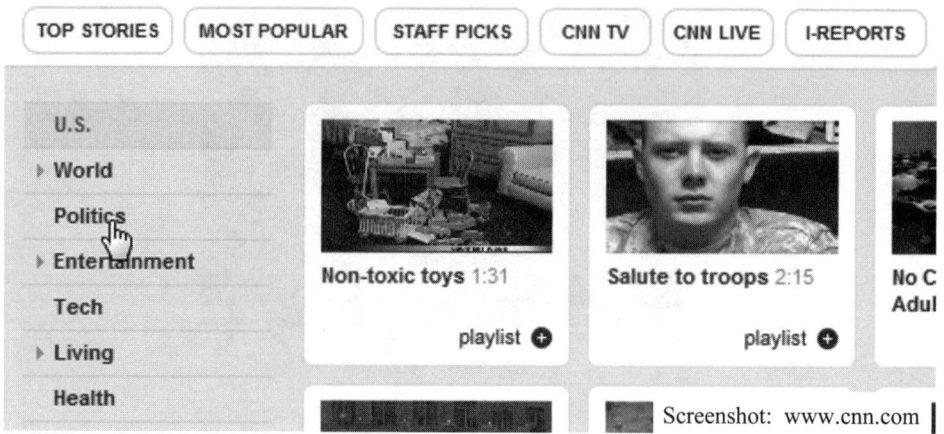

Screenshot: www.cnn.com |

26. Thumbnails of the political videos appear, together with short titles. Browse through the video clips and choose one or two that seem to be focused on the 2008 election. If possible, find a video on the strategic issues faced by the Democratic Party/candidate. Watch that video or videos. *On the worksheet, summarize the issue being discussed on the video and how it impacts the Democrats' chance in this election.* You have now learned some basics about what the Democrats stand for, and the challenges/opportunities they face in this election.

Done!

DEFINING THE DEMOCRATS WORKSHEET

1. What voter group targeted by the Democrats did you chose?

2. Why is it interesting that the Dems are reaching out to this group?

3. What are the Democrats doing to reach out to this group?

4. Summarize the Democratic position on the issue focused on in step 11 of this exercise.

5. Summarize Democratic thinking on the platform issue you chose.

6. Summarize the philosophy or policy idea presented by the Democratic presidential candidate in the speech you viewed.

7. Summarize what you learned from the CNN video.

ISSUE TWO
DEFINING THE REPUBLICANS

In this exercise, you will repeat many of the investigative strategies you used for Issue One. By the end of these first two exercises, you should have a better sense of how the two major parties differ (or not) on key issues and philosophies. You will also have a better sense of the strategic issues they face in presenting those ideas and philosophies in the 2008 election.

1. You will begin with an investigation of the kinds of people the Republicans target as likely supporters of their Party. Go to **www.gop.com.** You are now at one of the key homepages of the Republican Party. Explore the page all you wish to get a sense of Republican values. When you are done, return to the homepage.

2. To learn about key voter groups targeted by the Republicans, click on the link for **"GOP Teams"** on the homepage (top right of the page).

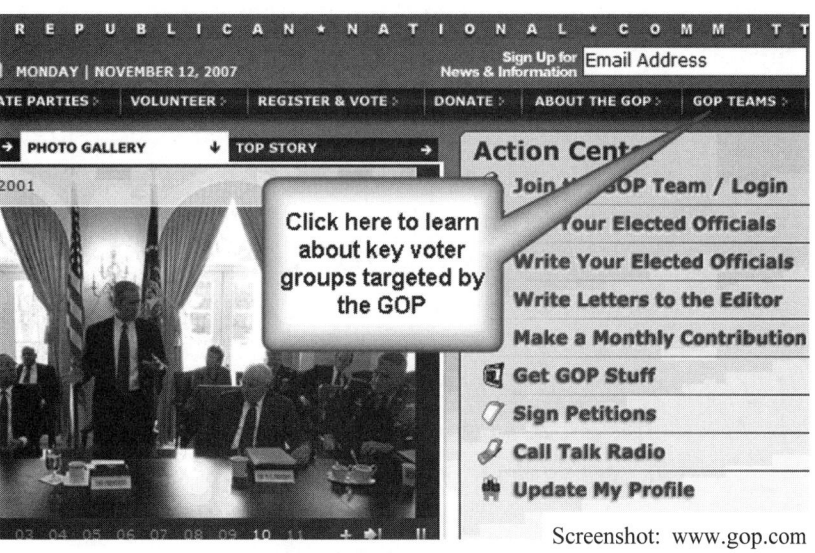

Screenshot: www.gop.com

3. You will be taken to a page listing several key voter groups targeted by the Republican Party. They are called "teams" on this page (for

example, the "Catholics Team" and the "Entrepreneurs Team"). You must scroll down the page to get to the listing of all the teams.

Screenshot: www.gop.com

4. In exercise one, you saw that the Democratic Party had a similar listing of key voter groups. You can remind yourself of the Democrats' list of groups by viewing the screenshot in step 2 of the previous exercise. You can also go to **www.democrats.org** and click on the **"people"** link to see the list again, which might help in the next step.

5. Compare the list of "teams" on the Republican website to the list of "people" on the Democratic website. *Come up with two voter groups that BOTH parties target. Also come up with a group that ONLY the Republicans target on their website, and a group that ONLY the Democrats target. Fill in the answers on your worksheet.*

6. *Do you feel that the **different** groups targeted by the parties reveal anything important about whom or what the party stands for? Fill in your brief answer on the worksheet.*

7. Examine the list of voter teams targeted by the GOP once again. *Based on this review, come up with one of these voter teams that is most interesting or surprising to you. On the attached worksheet, list that*

voter group and include a few sentences of analysis as to why it interests you that the Republicans are targeting this specific group.

8. **Now, click on your chosen voter group.** You are taken to the section of the website where the Republicans present information about why their party, rather than the Democratic Party, is the best to represent this group. The screenshot below focuses on the "Hispanic" voter team.

Hispanic Team Mission
In 1979, President Ronald Reagan said, "Hispanics are Republicans, don't know it yet." In 2005, President George W. Bush is proving Rea Screenshot: www.gop.com

9. Once you have pulled up the voter team you are interested in, you will see that the webpage offers a "team mission." It also offers links to articles of interest to that voter team, and provides other information on how the GOP is working on behalf of this group. Explore your chosen voter team page. *Fill out the worksheet with information about how the GOP is trying to reach out to and persuade this voter group.*

10. Now you will investigate some of the core issues and philosophies that the GOP is offering to the nation. Return to **www.gop.com.**

11. Move your cursor to the **"Issues"** section near the top of this web page (see screenshot on next page). A dropdown list appears to help you learn more about the GOP. **Click on one issue that interests you.**

Screenshot: www.gop.com

12. You are taken to a section of the website with details about the Republican position on this issue. Explore the materials that you find here to get a general sense of the Republican perspective on this issue.

13. *Based on what you learn there, go to the worksheet and include a short description of the Republican position on the issue you chose.*

14. For additional detail on Republican philosophy, you can explore the Party platform. Go to the homepage at **www.gop.com** and roll your cursor over the "**About the GOP**" option from the menu at the top. A list of buttons appears, including "**Party Platform.**" Click that link.

Screenshot: www.gop.com

15. The party platform appears. The platform is a thick document, and you won't be reading all of it. But you can learn about fundamental Republican values by perusing some of it. When the platform has opened, you will find an introduction and a Table of Contents, breaking the platform down into several themes (e.g., "Winning the War on Terror," and "Protecting Our Families"). Pick a theme that interests you (military and defense issues? Economic issues?). After you read the introduction, go to the section that deals with your issue.

16. *Read the section of the platform on the issue that interests you. Summarize Republican Party thinking on this issue on the worksheet.*

17. Now you can investigate how the Republican candidate for President thinks about the issues. Go to **www.gopconvention2008.com.** This is where the GOP provides information about their 2008 Convention.

18. Explore this page and you should find a link to a video of the keynote address of the Republican candidate. You can probably find it at the **"Convention Updates"** section (to the right of the page), or under the **"News"** button at the top of the page.

Screenshot: www.gopconvention2008.com. Used with permission.

19. Find the video of the candidate's speech. You do not need to watch the entire speech, but should watch at least 10 minutes of the speech to get a sense of some of the values and priorities of the Republican nominee.

20. *Use the worksheet to summarize a key issue/philosophy that this candidate is offering to the American people. If a video of the speech is not posted, you can read some of the "News" coverage on the GOP convention site to learn about key positions of the Republican nominee.*

21. Finally, you can investigate some strategic considerations that the Republicans must consider as they offer their ideas to the voters. To do this, repeat steps 23–26 of exercise one ("Defining the Democrats"). Only this time, when you come to the video list, choose one that looks like it focuses on challenges facing the Republican candidates.

22. Watch the video. *On the worksheet, summarize the issue being discussed and how it impacts the Republicans' chance in this election.*

Done!

DEFINING THE REPUBLICANS WORKSHEET

1. List two voter groups that both Democrats and Republicans target.

2. List a voter group that **only** the Democrats target:

3. List a voter group that **only** the Republicans target:

4. What conclusion can you offer about the significance of the **different** groups targeted by the two parties?

5. What voter group targeted by the GOP did you chose?

6. Why is it interesting that the GOP is reaching out to this group?

7. What is the GOP doing to reach out to this group?

8. Summarize GOP thinking in the platform on the issue you chose.

9. Summarize the philosophy or policy ideas presented by the GOP presidential candidate in the speech you viewed.

10. Summarize what you learned from the CNN video.

ISSUE THREE
PUBLIC OPINION: WHAT DO THE PEOPLE WANT?

"A campaign without polls is similar to a boat without oars...A campaign without polling is akin to hiking in the desert without a map." This is how Professor Richard Semiatin summarizes the reality that every major campaign today must rely on public opinion polls to help candidates understand and navigate the enduring political values and current political mood of the voters.[1] In addition to guiding political candidates as to the popular mood, polls help all citizens to understand what their neighbors are thinking about political issues. The editor of the famous Gallup poll calls public opinion polls a kind of "scientific gossip,"[2] helping us all to keep up with what the nation is thinking and allowing voters and candidates alike to answer such vital questions as "Who are we, as a people?", "What do we think about the state of the country?", and "What do we want our leaders to do?"

The previous exercises investigated the values and priorities of the two major parties, but it is also vital to know the values and priorities of the voters themselves. In large part, election outcomes are determined by the interaction between the values and goals of the voters and the values and goals of the candidates. The public has opinions—and any serious candidate must pay attention to them.

Even 100 years ago, famous scholars like James Bryce noted that the American people were famous for "freely and constantly reading, talking and judging of public affairs with a view to voting thereon."[3] More recently, V.O. Key has called public opinion a kind of "opinion dike" that channels election dynamics and the ideas of candidates within a fixed range, forcing officials and candidates not to stray too far from the values of their people.[4]

What are the values and policy goals of the American people as they face the 2008 election? In this exercise, you will investigate the structure of public opinion that candidates must deal with as they run their campaigns.

You will learn about important national databases like the American National Election Studies, and about places where you can find compendiums of current opinion polls. You will learn about some of the enduring values of the American people and will also investigate the voters' opinion on current policy issues. Throughout the exercise, you will be exploring the same kinds of polls that candidates and consultants look at when crafting their campaign strategies. Just like these political insiders, you will investigate the key issues in public opinion that each party should be aware of as it seeks victory in 2008.

---

[1] Richard Semiatin. *Campaigns in the 21st Century.* (Boston: McGraw-Hill, 2005) pp. 101, 125.

[2] Frank Newport, *Polling Matters* (New York: Time-Warner, 2004) p. x.

[3] James Bryce, from The American Commonwealth. In *The Lanahan Readings in the American Polity*, edited by Ann G. Serow and Everett C. Ladd (Baltimore: Lanahan Publishers, 2000). p. 325.

[4] V.O. Key, from Public Opinion and American Democracy. In The *Lanahan Readings in the American Polity*, edited by Ann G. Serow and Everett C. Ladd (Baltimore: Lanahan Publishers, 2000). p. 334.

PUBLIC OPINION:
WHAT DO THE PEOPLE WANT?

1. You will begin by investigating the underlying/enduring values and political identities of the American people. In these first steps you will examine voters' thoughts on their own political identity (are most people conservative, liberal, or neither?), their opinions about the political parties (do they feel warm or cold toward the Democrats and Republicans?), and their thoughts on some important policy issues. Instead of focusing on how voters feel about such issues at this single moment in time (fall of 2008), the initial steps in this exercise will help you investigate how voters' ideas and sentiments have changed or not changed over the last several decades.

2. Go to **www.electionstudies.org**. You are now at the website of the American National Election Studies (ANES). This website provides access to some of the most sophisticated and well-respected public opinion, voting and public participation data in America. The data is generated largely through extensive polling during presidential election years, and is made available for free, with National Science Foundation support, to scholars across the nation.

3. This website has all sorts of publications and reports that you can view, and datasets that you can interact with to create your own reports. For this exercise, you will only look at one section of the website: the "Guide to Public Opinion," where ANES provides prepared graphs and tables based on their polling data.

4. Click on **"Guide to Public Opinion,"** among the menu options to the left of the screen (see screenshot on next page).

☑ANES
American National Election Studies

recent site c

64 DAYS LEFT to submit proposals	☑ **What is ANES?** The American National Election Studies (ANES) produ quality data on voting, public opinion, and political parti serve the research needs of social scientists, teachers policy makers and journalists who want to better under theoretical and empirical foundations of national electi Central to this mission is the active involvement of the research community in all phases of the project. Read
Data Center Download data and documentation.	
Future Data Collections Details about upcoming surveys.	☑ **Only 70 Days Left!** There are only 70 days left to propose content for the 2 National Election Studies (ANES) Time Series Study! Ir pre-election and post-election interviews will be collect with a new, nationally-representative sample, continuin presidential year time series that has been conducted
Online Commons Submit your question proposals.	
Guide to Public Opinion Graphs and tables using ANES data.	Content will be from three sources: 1. previous ANES T questionnaires; 2. proposals received via the ANES On Commons; and 3. proposals received via the ANES Bo program. Read More...
Reference Library Publications, p	Screenshot: www.electionstudies.org. Used with permission.

5. You are taken to the ANES guide on how American values and behaviors have or have not changed over time. There is a menu of topics, as seen in screenshot below.

The ANES Guide to Public Opinion and Electoral Behavior

The *Guide* provides immediate access to tables and graphs that display the ebb and flow of pul electoral behavior, and choice in American politics over time. It serves as a resource for politica policy makers, and journalists, teachers, students, and social scientists.

The *Guide* currently contains data from 1948 through 2004.
Displays in the *Guide* are organized into nine topics:

1. Social and Religious **Characteristics of the Electorate** (such as age, race, gender, education, and religion)
2. Partisanship **and Evaluation of the Political Parties**
3. Ideological **Self-Identification**
4. Public Opinion **on Public Policy Is** Screenshot: www.electionstudies.org (such as health care, affirmative action, abortion, the military, and the economy)
5. Support **for the Political System** (such as trust in government and government responsiveness)

6. You will explore some of the polls under topics 2 (Partisanship), 3 (Ideological Self-Identification) and 4 (Public Opinion on Public Policy Issues). Click on the link for **topic 2: "Partisanship."**

7. You are taken to a page with links to charts on Partisanship issues. You should note that other topics (e.g., Ideological Self-Identification, Public Opinion on Public Policy Issues, etc.) are also listed on this same page, together with links to charts, if you scroll down the page.

8. You will first investigate how partisanship (that is, Americans' tendency to think of themselves as Democrats, Republicans, or as something else) has or has not changed over the years. Click on the link for **Table 2A.1: "Party Identification 7-Point Scale."**

2. Partisanship and Evaluation of the Political Parties

2.A. Partisanship

- Table 2A.1. Party Identification 7-Point Scale
- Table 2A.2. Party Identification 3-Point Scale
- Table 2A.3. Strength of Partisanship

> Click this link to go to the table

2.B. Evaluation of the Parties

- Table 2B.1. Average Feelings Toward Parties
- Table 2B.2. Average Feeling Thermometer Rating Toward Parties
- Table 2B.3. Which Party Best Able to Handle Most Important Problem
- Table 2B.4. Important Differences Between 2 Parties
- Table 2B.5. Is One Party More C Screenshot: www.electionstudies.org

9. A table appears, breaking Americans down into categories, such as "Strong Democrat," "Weak Democrat," "Strong Republican," "Weak Republican," "Independent," etc. This data was gathered by ANES by polling thousands of Americans every two years since 1952.

10. Examine this table and pay attention to the data from 1952 to 1960 (titled '52 and '60), and the 2000 to 2004 period ('00 to '04). Based on this analysis, draw conclusions as to at least one category of voters that generally has stayed the same since the 1950s, one category that

significantly has shrunk since the 1950s, and one category that has grown since the 1950s. *Include your answers on the worksheet.*

11. Based on this data, would you say that voters since the 1950s have become more Democratic in their loyalties, more Republican, or more independent? *Include this answer on the worksheet.*

12. You have investigated how voters describe their own partisan position, otherwise known as their support for one party or the other. It is also important to know if voters feel there are important differences between the parties, or not. Do voters believe it matters whether they vote for Republicans or Democrats in terms of policy outcomes?

13. To examine this question, return to the list of graphs you went to in steps 6–8. Click on **Table 2B.4: "Important Differences Between 2 Parties"**.

14. You are taken to a table that shows the percent of voters over the years who say there are "No important differences" between the parties and the percent of voters saying "Yes, there are important differences." (The "N" at the bottom of the chart is the number of voters surveyed)

Important Difference in What Democratic and Republican

	'52	'54	'56	'58	'60	'62	'64	'66	'68	'70	'72	'74	'76	'78
No Difference :	41	**	**	**	43	**	44	56	44	**	44	**	42	**
Yes, a Difference :	50	**	**	**	50	**	55	40	52	**	46	**	47	**
Don't Know, Depends:	9	**	**	**	6	**	1	4	4	**	10	**	10	**
N	1757				1818		14							

Screenshot: www.electionstudies.org

15. President George W. Bush was elected in 2000 and in 2004. Examine this chart, and compare voter sentiments in those two election years (called '00 and '04 in this chart) to voter sentiments in most years prior to this. *Do voters in more recent years feel that party differences are becoming more or less important than they did in most previous years? Include this answer on your worksheet. Why do you think voters feel this way? On the worksheet, provide a brief explanation of the voter opinion data from 2000 and 2004 that you see in this chart.*

16. This data also allows you to investigate voter opinions on vital policy issues over the years. One important issue is whether voters feel that the government should increase spending on social programs (like education, health care, and roads) or whether the government should cut spending and shrink its size. Examine how voters feel on this issue by returning to the list of tables and clicking on the link to **Table 4A.5: "Government Services and Spending"**.

Government Services and Spending 1982-2004

	'82	'84	'86	'88	'90	'92	'94	'96	'98	'00
Cut Services/Spending 1 :	9	6	5	5	4	5	9	6	6	4
2 :	10	9	6	8	6	8	11	10	8	5
3 :	13	13	13	13	12	13	16	15	12	9
4 :	23	26	25	23	24	26	24	25	26	25
5 :	11	14	17	14	15	15	16	15	16	18
6 :	6	8	12	10	11	8	6	7	13	11
More Services/Spending 7:	7	7	12	7	11	7	5	5	11	10
DK, Haven't Thought :	20	16	9	20	17	19	13	16	9	17
N	1404	2229	2168							

Screenshot: www.electionstudies.org

17. In this chart, people picking 5, 6, or 7 felt that the government should spend *more* on public services, with 7 representing people wanting the largest growth in spending. People choosing 1, 2 or 3 wanted the government to *cut* spending and services, with 1 representing the people who wanted the largest cuts. This is important data, because Democrats tend to propose new government services and spending, while Republicans propose to cut taxes, spending and government programs. What do you learn about how voter opinion on this issue has changed since 1982? Did more people in 2004 want government spending and services to go up or down, compared to the early 1980s? *Include your answer on your worksheet.*

18. Now that you have identified some historic public values on such things as party affiliation and the desire for more or less government

spending, you can move on to investigating more timely/current public opinion: how do voters *today* feel?

19. Go to **www.pollingreport.com**. You can see a long list of categories of polls to explore. Each of these categories presents polling data from a variety of national polling sources.

20. Examine polling data found in three categories: "Direction of the Country," "National Priorities," and "Iraq" (see screenshot below).

Screenshot: www.pollingreport.com. Used with permission.

21. Click on the link for **"Direction of the country."** These polls describe whether voters feel the country is headed in the right or wrong direction. If most people feel the country is headed in the wrong direction, it is usually bad news for the party which controls the presidency (in this case, the Republicans). If people say the country is one the right track, it is good for the party in control of the presidency.

22. Examine the last several months of data on this poll. Would you say that this data is good or bad for the Republican candidate for the presidency? Why? *Include your short answer on the worksheet.*

23. Now click the link for **"National Priorities"** (under the State of the Union category). The polls you see here inform you as to what the voters feel are the most important issues facing the country. *Based on these polls, what would you say are the three most important issues facing voters this year? List these issues on your worksheet.*

24. Now click the link for **"Iraq,"** under the National Security category. You get a variety of polls about whether people approve or disapprove of the way President Bush is handling Iraq, whether people feel Iraq was worth the American effort, etc. Look over these polls, and come up with one piece of data that you think will be important to the election (for example, you might find that most people feel that the Democrats have been too hasty in pushing for withdrawal from Iraq). *On the worksheet, summarize this fact and why you think it is important.*

25. Return to the list of all polls at the homepage of **pollingreport.com.** You will notice that there are many polls under the categories called **"In the News"** and **"Issues."** Pick an issue that is interesting to you in one of these categories (for example, you might pick "the federal deficit," "abortion," "immigration," "taxes" or any other such issue).

26. **Click on the link to that issue** and examine the polls you find. Draw a conclusion about how opinion on that issue might influence the election. *On the worksheet, summarize what the data teaches about this issue. You could summarize what voters want their leaders to do on this issue; or you might summarize why one or the other presidential candidates is likely to do better on this issue.*

27. Finally, on the bottom right hand side of the pollingreport.com homepage, there is a section called "Random Samples." This section has sample news articles and analysis focused on the meaning of various polls. Click on the link to the **"Random Samples"** section to be taken to short summaries of each of these articles (see screenshot on the next page). Choose one or two articles that interest you and read them in more detail, seeking to learn more about the state of public opinion today.

Issues
Abortion
Energy
Environment
Gun laws
Health policy *11/29*
Immigration
Same-sex marriage
Social Security
Stem cell research
Taxes
More issues . . .

Details on accessing STATE polls

G.W. Bush On Immigration.
Answer To Bush View On Immigration
From Return Of The Gods Web Site!

Ads by Google

11/01   11/03   11/05   11/07
11/02   11/04   11/06

pollingreport.com

More graphics:
• National Barometer • Poll Gallery

Random Samples *12*
Candidates woo California huge
absentee vote • Clinton as Support
of Los Angeles. Amplifying Voting
From Abroad • Iraq: Survey of
Reporters on the Front Lines • Iowa
Caucuses a Challenge for Pollsters •
Consumer Comfort Hits Two-Year Low
• Public Sees Progress in War Effort •
Politics of Race and Religion • Tax
dollars went to political polls • MORE
...

Screenshot: www.pollingreport.com.
Used with permission.

28. *On the worksheet, summarize what you learned about public opinion from this "Random Samples" reading.*

Done!

INVESTIGATING PUBLIC OPINION WORKSHEET

1. List a category of partisan voters (for example, "strong Democrat" or "Independent") that has stayed generally the same size since the 1950s.

2. List a category of voters that has shrunk since the 1950s.

3. List a category of voters that has grown since the 1950s.

4. Overall, have voters since the 1950s become more Democratic, more Republican, or more independent in their self-identification?

5. Did voters in 2000-2004 feel that differences between the two parties were becoming more or less important than previously?

6. Why do you think voters felt as you described them in question 5?

7. Did voters in 2004 want government spending and services to go up or down, compared to how they felt in the early 1980s?

8. Do voters feel the country is going in the right or wrong direction? How might this opinion affect the Republican candidate?

9. What do voters say are the three most important issues today?

10. How might voter opinions on Iraq effect the election?

11. What issue did you choose in step 25-26 of the exercise and what did the polls teach you about how voters feel on this issue?

12. What did you learn from the "Random Samples" article?

The Daisy Girl Ad. Reagan and the Bear. It's Morning Again in America. The Willie Horton Ad. The Swift Boat Ad. These are among the most influential and remembered television ads in American political history. These ads are commonly no more than 30 seconds long, and yet they are often credited with tremendous influence in determining the winning candidate. The television ad "air war" is a vital part of election 2008, and in years to come we will probably remember one or two of this year's ads as so powerful that they will enter the campaign ad "hall of fame," together with the ads listed above.

Which of today's campaign ads will rise to the stature of such memorable and influential forces? There will be many to choose from. The Center for Responsive Politics, one of the nation's leading sources of campaign finance data, estimates that this year's presidential election will shatter previous election spending records. At least $1 billion dollars will be contributed directly to the presidential candidates, and billions more will be spent by local and state parties, independent groups and other election candidates running for office.[1] Much of this money will be spent on television advertising, otherwise known as the "air war." The TNS Media Intelligence/Campaign MediaAnalysis Group has estimated that over $3 billion will be spent on television ads to influence the 2008 election—about twice as much as was spent in 2004.[2]

Candidates, parties and independent groups spend this kind of money because they know it matters. Voters see these ads over and over, and they receive endless replay on the news stations, YouTube, and the like. With so much playtime, the ads are likely to have an effect on the voters. The famous "Willie Horton" ad from 1988 is widely credited with permanently shifting momentum from Democratic candidate Dukakis to Republican candidate George Bush. And every election observer is well-versed in how the "Swift boat" ads of 2004 helped doom the Kerry campaign. Those ads have even resulted in an informal word that is now used to describe powerful, negative advertising attacks on the record or character of a candidate: *"Swiftboating."* No candidate wants to be "swiftboated" and every candidate seeks an ad that will lead voters to feel that the candidate represents "morning again in America," just as Ronald Reagan's famous 1984 ads did.

In this exercise, you will view some of the most famous campaign ads in American history, and will assess what it is about those ads that made them so effective. You will also view a set of ads running in the current election, and will choose a positive and negative ad to analyze in some detail. With new Internet technology, more and more video campaigning is done beyond the boundaries of traditional television campaign ads, and you will also analyze a bit of this alternative video coverage, produced by independent groups and running on the Net. Finally, you will even have the opportunity to explore some of the tricks of the trade as you design your own campaign ad, complete with ominous music and threatening voice-overs!

---

[1] Data available at www.opensecrets.org/pres08/index.asp (accessed November 24, 2007).
[2] Mark Preston. "Political Television Advertising to Reach $3 Billion." CNN News. October 15, 2007, www.cnn.com/2007/POLITICS/10/15/ad.spending/index.html (accessed November 24, 2007).

INVESTIGATING CAMPAIGN ADS

1. You will begin your investigation of television campaign advertising by examining some of the most influential campaign ads in history.

2. Go to **http://livingroomcandidate.movingimage.us/**.

3. You are now at "The Living Room Candidate" archive—the on-line campaign ad archive of the Museum of the Moving Image (a museum collecting moving image footage throughout American history). You can click on the "featured ad" to watch the currently highlighted historical ad. You can read about the history and strategies of campaign television advertising in the text below the featured ad. Most important to this exercise, to the left of the page is a list of links that you can click to see campaign ads from elections going back to 1952.

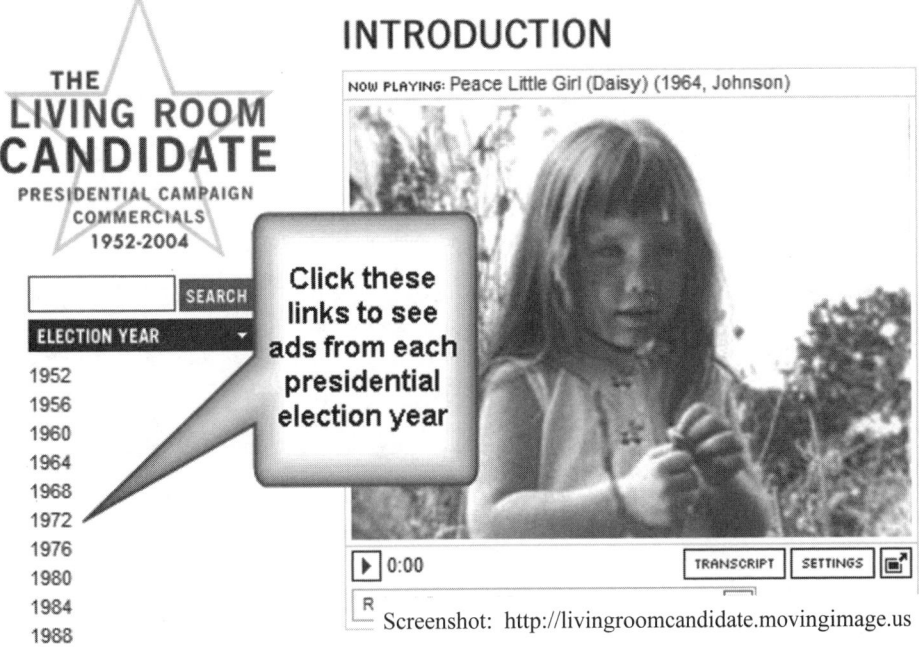

Screenshot: http://livingroomcandidate.movingimage.us

4. As you view ads from various years in the following steps, keep in mind that when you are done, you will further analyze the one ad that you found most effective among all the historical ads that you viewed.

5. Begin by examining a famous ad from 1964: The Daisy Girl ad. This ad played on the fact that the Republican candidate for president, Barry Goldwater, had suggested using nuclear weapons in the Vietnam War and other conflicts. The ad suggests that Goldwater would be a trigger-happy military hothead, with his hand on the nuclear button.

6. **Click the link to the 1964 election ads to the left of the screen.** You will be taken to a page with thumbnails of various "Democratic" and "Republican" ads from the 1964 election. You can also read a short overview of election dynamics from this year at the bottom of the page.

7. From the thumbnail pictures to the right of the screen, under the Democratic column, find the ad labeled **"Peace Little Girl"** (otherwise called the "Daisy Girl" ad). Click on it to view the ad. As you roll over each ad, you can see its title in the gray bar above the ads.

1964 JOHNSON vs. GOLDWATER

Screenshot: http://livingroomcandidate.movingimage.us. © Museum of the Moving Image. Used with permission.

8. If your computer has trouble loading and playing the ad, try changing the settings by clicking **"settings,"** as in the screenshot below. Try a variety of settings to find what works.

1964 JOHNSON vs. GOLDWATER

Screenshot: http://livingroomcandidate.movingimage.us.
© Museum of the Moving Image. Used with permission.

9. When you finish viewing the ad, think through what makes this ad memorable. Why do you think this ad is remembered as having a significant an impact on the election? Think about such things as:

    *   Did the ad manipulate/distort images of candidates or other things to influence the voters' perceptions?
    *   Is music used to influence voters?
    *   Is the voice/tone of the narrator used to influence voters?
    *   Is the ad a negative attack on the character of a candidate?
    *   Is the ad a celebration of the character or ideas of a candidate?
    *   Does the ad play on strong human emotions like fear of death or crime, racial hostility, or love of country and family?
    *   Does the ad effectively use humor to sell its point?

10. Now move on to the 1984 election. You will view two famous Ronald Reagan campaign ads. Click the **"1984"** election link in the list of election years, as seen in the screenshot under point 2 above. When the list of 1984 election ads appears, search under the "Republican" column of thumbnails for the ad titled **"Prouder, Stronger, Better"** (it will be the first ad in the list). View the ad. This ad (often called

the "Morning in America" ad) played on the fact that the American economy under President Reagan from 1980 to 1984 seemed to be improving from when Democratic President Carter presided over such economic problems as high inflation and high unemployment. The ad celebrates the spirit of national recovery that Reagan's team wanted voters to associate with Ronald Reagan.

11. When you are done viewing this ad, search for the ad titled **"Bear"**: it is the fourth ad in the list. This ad sought to remind Americans that even though America hadn't recently been in direct conflict with the Soviet Union, the Soviet "bear" was still very dangerous, and that America needed a strong military leader, just in case. View the ad.

12. As in step 9, ponder what makes these ads memorable and effective.

13. Now move on to the 1988 election. You will view two influential Republican ads. Repeat the steps you followed for previous election years and find the **"Tank Ride"** ad (ad number six in the Republican column) and the **"Willie Horton"** ad (ad number nine in the Republican column). The screenshot on the next page points out these ads. Before you view the ads, you might want to read the short **"overview"** section, right below the ad viewer, to get a better understanding of the times during which the ad was playing.

The "Tank Ride" ad features Governor Dukakis riding around in a military tank, and looking somewhat silly. Here, you can see the Bush team arguing that Dukakis would be an ineffective and weak military leader, and subtly reminding voters of the Republican argument that Democrats can't be trusted on national defense.

The "Willie Horton" ad highlights criminal justice issues in Massachusetts while Dukakis was Governor. Playing on the Democrats' reputation for being "soft on crime," the ad argues that a Dukakis presidency would make all Americans less safe in their own homes.

14. When you are done viewing the ads, think about what makes them memorable and effective.

1988 BUSH vs. DUKAKIS

Screenshot: http://livingroomcandidate.movingimage.us.
© Museum of the Moving Image. Used with permission.

15. Finally, you will view two famous ads from the 2004 election: the "Swift Boat" ads. These ads are remembered as playing a key role in Kerry's loss to Bush in 2004. The context of the ads was that Kerry was running as a Vietnam War hero, a soldier who had received two purple hearts and achieved distinction in combat. Based partly on this history, Kerry was offering himself, in America's time of war in Iraq, as an alternative to George W. Bush, who had never served in combat. The anti-Kerry Swift boat ads were produced to undermine Kerry's military record. They were not produced by the Republican Party, nor by candidate George W. Bush's team, but by a fully independent

group ("Swift Boat Veterans for Truth"), seeking to influence the election.

16. To find ads by such independent groups, you need to click on the button called **"The Desktop Candidate"** to the left of the webpage, underneath the list of years. This will take you away from the television ads produced by the parties and candidates, to a different section of advertisements produced by independent groups, or that were produced for the Internet.

Screenshot: http://livingroomcandidate.movingimage.us. © Museum of the Moving Image. Used with permission.

17. Among the options under the **"Desktop Candidate"** is a **"Shadow Campaign"** link. Click there to go to ads by independent groups.

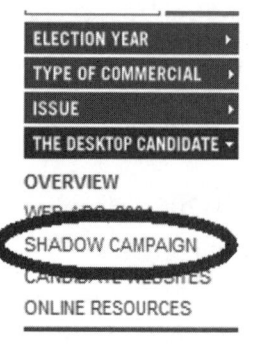 

Screenshot: http://livingroomcandidate.movingimage.us. © Museum of the Moving Image. Used with permission.

18. A list of ads appears. Find and view the two ads sponsored by a group called "Swift Boat Veterans for Truth" (they are toward the bottom of the list of ads). The ad titles are **"Any Questions"** and **"Sellout."** Think about why these ads were so harmful to the Kerry campaign.

19. You have now viewed some of the most memorable ads of the last forty years. Choose the ad you find the most effective and/or interesting. *On the worksheet, name this ad and provide a summary of*

why you find the ad to be so memorable or effective. In your answer, you may want to consider some of the points raised in step 9, above.

20. Before you explore the ads that are running in the current campaign, you can practice building your own campaign ad—an amusing diversion that will alert you to some of the tricks of the trade to watch for in today's ads. Go to **www.pbs.org/30secondcandidate/.**

21. This is the website of a PBS program on historic campaign ads. For this exercise, you are interested in the menu item called **"Tricks of the Trade."** Click on it to build your own campaign ad.

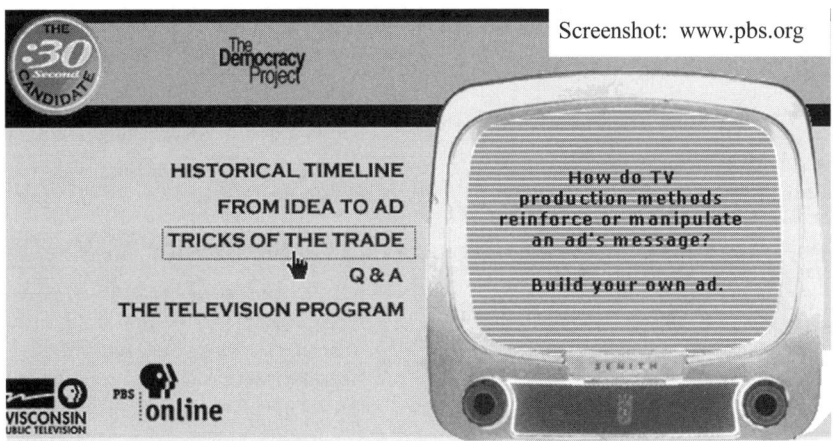

Screenshot: www.pbs.org

22. Follow the directions to craft different campaign ads from the exact same film footage. It should heighten your awareness of the techniques being utilized in ads you are seeing during this campaign season.

23. Now you are ready to carefully examine campaign ads running in the current presidential election. A good archive of current ads is maintained in the "Campaign Toolbox" at the Washington Post. Go to it at **www.washingtonpost.com/politics.**

24. This page has numerous resources for following the election. The **"Campaign 2008 Toolbox"** link should be in a section called **"The Presidential Field,"** as in the screenshot on the next page. Scroll down the page looking for the **Campaign 2008 Toolbox** link. Click it.

THE CHARLIE ROSE INTERVIEWS
- 📹 Bill Richardson
- 📹 Mike Huckabee

THE PRESIDENTIAL FIELD
- Today's Events | Candidates | Issues Tracker
- Campaign Fi~~~~~ Primaries / Caucuses
- Campaign 2008 Toolbox

CONGRESS VOTES DATABASE
- Recent Votes: House | Senate

» More Headlines: More news fr(
House, Congress and the feder;

Screenshot: www.washingtonpost.com

25. You are taken to a set of tools for following the election. The ones you will use are in the "Multi-media Coverage" section. They are the "Mixed Messages" tool (taking you to an archive of current campaign ads) and the "Channel '08" tool (taking you to video clips of different aspects of the campaign). See the screenshot below.

- 'Candidate Collection' Widget - Add candidates to your blog or Facebook page.
- Events Tracker - Follow the candidates' campaigns across the country.
- Live Discussions - Talk with candidates live or read their discussion transcripts.

CALENDARS

- The FastTrack Campaign - Keep track of shifting primary dates and delegate counts.

POLLS

Screenshot: www.washingtonpost.com
- Politics Glossary - Political terms defined and deciphered.

MULTIMEDIA COVERAGE

- Post.com Multimedia - Photo and video coverage of the campaign.
- Channel '08 - Analysis of political video.
- Mixed Messages - Campaign ads organized by candidate and issue.

ISSUES

26. Click on the link for **"Mixed Messages."** You are taken to a list of current campaign ads, organized by such things as issue, candidate, and even background music. Spend some time exploring and viewing these ads, in whatever categories are interesting to you.

27. In your explorations, find one ad that you judge to be a powerful and positive ad—an ad that celebrates a particular candidate, and/or that leaves voters feeling positive and upbeat about a particular issue or party. *Provide the ad title on the worksheet (the title is above the ad on the computer viewer as you watch it). Summarize why this ad is so effective. Was it the use of images, the playing of music, or the sharing of positive facts and ideas in the ad that most struck you?*

28. Repeat this process for a negative or "attack" ad (there is a category called "attack" ads at the bottom of the list of ad categories on this website). Find a strong ad that attacks the politics or character of another candidate or political party, and that leaves the voter feeling upset, angry or fearful. *Provide the ad title, and explain the effectiveness of the ad on the worksheet as you did in the previous step.*

29. Viewing the TV ads of presidential campaigns and independent groups is one way that voters can learn about the candidates. But in recent years, there has been an explosion of Internet video coverage of political issues—represented by such websites as YouTube, where voters can directly post their own video clips and analysis. Some of these independent sites are altering the dynamics of the election, and they are interesting places to find alternative coverage of the election.

30. Three good sites for alternative video coverage of the election are:

    • **The Washington Post "Channel '08" link.** Follow it through the instructions in step 25 of this exercise, above. This site partners with the prezvid.com site listed below.

    • **www.prezvid.com.** This site provides election video clips and analysis from a wide range of sources, including some video posted directly by voters themselves.

    • **www.youtube.com/youchoose.** This site organizes video clips of the candidates, organized by issue and candidate. Links to related videos posted by users are also provided.

31. Choose at least one of these links to explore in some detail, viewing some of the videos you find there. Draw conclusions about whether this new form of independent video journalism is useful to voters or not. How do these videos teach voters things about the election and the candidates that go beyond campaign ads and the evening news—or do they? *Summarize your thoughts on the worksheet.*

32. One final issue to explore is what comedian Steven Colbert would call the "truthiness" of the campaign ads. Voters see dozens, perhaps hundreds, of campaign ads in an election season, shaping the way they see the candidates, and sometimes determining their final vote. But what is true and informative in these ads, and what is false and distorting? One way to explore the honesty of campaign ads is the new website by the St. Petersburg Times and Congressional Quarterly. Go to **www.politifact.com.**

33. Here you can explore a vast database of candidate statements during debates, speeches, interviews, television ads and more. As reported on the site, "every day, reporters and researchers...will analyze the candidates' speeches, TV ads and interviews and determine whether the claims are accurate." The menu at the top of the page lets you explore articles on candidates' honesty and deception, examine the "truth-o-meter" which reports on a honesty of candidate statements, and open the "attack file" archives, assessing the honesty of political attacks, and more.

Screenshot: www.politifact.com. Used with permission.

34. For this exercise, you will only explore the honesty of a few sample television ads. Scroll down this webpage, looking on the right hand side for a section called "**Browse.**" You want to find a collection of links under the "**Browse the Truth-O-Meter**" label. In that section, click on the link for "**By where they said it**" (see screenshot on the next page).

Browse

Browse the Truth-O-Meter:
- By candidate or attacker
- By our ruling
- By subject
- By political party
- By where they said it
- Pants on Fire rulings

Click here to find the campaign ads

Contribute

No, we don't want to take your money. But we are more than willing to listen if you know of any facts or story ideas for the Truth-O-Meter. *truthometer@politifact.com*

Screenshot: www.politifact.com. Used with permission.

35. A list of "Forums" appears. You can search for candidate statements based on where they made them (e.g., a debate, an interview, or a campaign speech). Scroll down this list and click on **"TV Ad."**

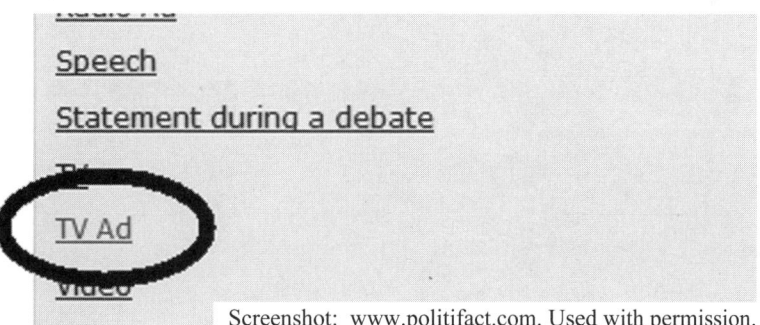

Speech

Statement during a debate

TV Ad

Screenshot: www.politifact.com. Used with permission.

36. A list of TV ads appears, together with the Truth-O-Meter rating of their honesty. Select at least two ads to view—one rated "True" or "Mostly True," and one rated "Half-True" or less. To view the analysis of the ad, and the ad itself, click on the **"Details"** link at the bottom of the ad's description (see screenshot on next page).

Statements by TV Ad

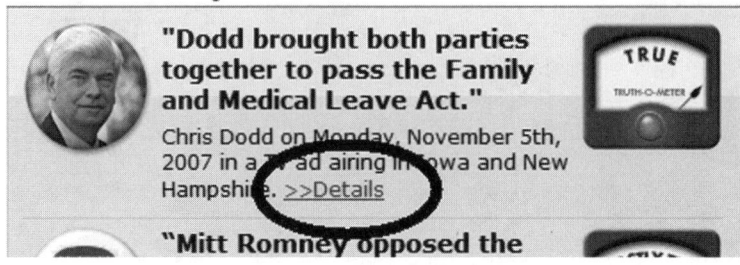

"Dodd brought both parties together to pass the Family and Medical Leave Act."

Chris Dodd on Monday, November 5th, 2007 in a TV ad airing in Iowa and New Hampshire. >>Details

"Mitt Romney opposed the

Screenshot: www.politifact.com. Used with permission.

37. A short analysis of the "truthiness" of the ad appears. You can view the ad itself by clicking on the video link to the right of the analysis.

38. After reading the analysis and viewing the ads, think over whether the "fact-checking" at this kind of website can be expected to influence the election in any way. *Share your conclusions on the worksheet.*

Done!

INVESTIGATING CAMPAIGN ADS WORKSHEET

1. Which of the historical ads did you find most memorable?

2. Briefly explain why you think that ad was so memorable/effective.

3. What was the title of the current "positive" ad that you found to be effective? Also briefly summarize the reasons for your conclusion.

4.   What was the title of the current "negative" ad that you found to be effective? Also summarize the reasons for your conclusion.

5.   Do you think the "new" form of independent video journalism (i.e., YouTube videos) teaches voters important lessons that go beyond campaign ads and the evening news—or not? Why or why not?

6.   Do you think the data and analysis on websites like PolitiFact.com can make a difference in the election? Why or why not?

In 2000, it all came down to Florida. In 2004, Ohio proved decisive. Beyond these two states, only a handful of closely contested states like Pennsylvania, New Mexico and Missouri drew the attention of presidential campaigns. Some of the most populated states like California and New York were all but ignored by candidates competing for victory. The fact that campaign strategists commonly spend more time fretting over tiny New Mexico than vast California is due to the Electoral College system.

Instead of relying on the direct vote of the people to determine the president, the Electoral College awards votes to candidates based on who wins the popular vote in each state. For the most part, states deliver their votes in a *winner-take-all* system: whoever wins the majority of the popular vote in each state wins ALL of that state's electoral votes. California, for example, gives its entire cache of 55 electoral votes to the state's popular vote winner, so the tens of millions of votes cast for the other candidate are discarded in determining the Electoral College winner.

The winner-take-all Electoral College system has profound effects on how elections are waged. In a system based directly on the popular vote, it would make sense for candidates to spend a great deal of time competing in heavily populated states like California and Texas—smaller states like New Mexico and Iowa would not see the sustained campaign attention they often see today. Furthermore, states themselves wouldn't even matter in a direct election system: candidates could wage broad national campaigns and attract voters from all corners in building a winning national majority. How the majority of voters in Oregon or Kentucky voted would not be important—only the final national total would matter.

In the winner-take-all Electoral College, however, candidates win votes based on state-by-state voter majorities, so candidates MUST focus on winning individual states, not just on the national tally. Moreover, candidates must focus on states that they have a chance of winning, and mostly ignore the rest. If a state is a sure victory for one party or the other (often called "safe states" or "base states"), it doesn't make sense for candidates to spend resources competing there. Instead, candidates must determine which states are truly up for grabs (called "'battleground" or "swing" states) and must spend most of their effort there. That is why heavily populated states like New York and California are often abandoned by Republican candidates (Democrats always win these states in recent presidential elections) while Texas is mostly ignored by the Democrats. Meanwhile, sparsely populated New Mexico and Iowa receive attention by campaign strategists as these states are more up for grabs.

Because campaigns must win a coalition of individual states, strategists must identify which states are safe for their party, which states are hopeless, and which states are competitive. Since campaigns have limited resources, they must target a limited number of winnable states, avoid their opponent's base states and even ignore some swing states, in order to focus only on the most promising states that will help the campaign win at least 270 electoral votes—a majority of the Electoral College.

In this exercise, you will begin to build a strategy for the candidate of your choice to win at least 270 votes in the Electoral College, and thus, win the presidency. You will examine the historical patterns and current polling data in order to determine which states fall into the category of each party's "base states" and "swing states" (states that are unpredictable in which way they will vote). You will investigate the history, polling results, and demographics of states so that you can define which states are safe for your party and which are battleground states. In the exercise that follows, you will decide which of those battleground states especially to target.

THE ELECTORAL COLLEGE BATTLEGROUND

1. Your first step in building a winning Electoral College strategy is to define each party's base states, so that you don't waste resources in states that are impossible to win or that are sure bets for your party. Base states (otherwise known as "safe states") are states that one or the other major party should win easily, based on historical performance and current polling, and thus are states in which neither party needs to invest much time or resources competing.

2. To define your "base states," you will begin with an examination of historical voting patterns of states in the Electoral College, in order to gain a sense of long term political dynamics. Begin by going to **www.270towin.com**. This website provides an "Electoral College calculator"— a tool to examine past election results and to map one's own Electoral College predictions and strategies.

3. At this site, you will examine presidential elections since 1928—an era that takes us from the historic elections of Franklin Roosevelt to the present. Understanding Electoral College trends will help you learn how today's "base" and "swing" states have evolved as they have.

Screenshot: www.270towin.com. Used with permission.

4. Using the drop down menu, **select the 1928 presidential election**. States that Republicans won are colored red and Democratic states are colored blue. *On your worksheet, note a region of the country that remained Democratic even as Republicans swept the nation in 1928.*

5. **Now select the 1932 election.** This was FDR's first victory, a landslide that occurred in the midst of the Great Depression, for which the Republicans paid a price in the election. *On your worksheet, note a region that remained Republican in the midst of the Democratic sweep.*

6. **Now examine the electoral results in 1936, 1940 and 1944** (President Roosevelt's other three victories). Which party generally drew its strength from the Northern states and which party drew more strength from Southern states? *Include your answer on the worksheet.*

7. You may have heard the phrase "Solid South," which in electoral terms meant that Southern states were dependable ("solid") Democratic base states from the 1880s forward (post–Civil War and Reconstruction), for almost 100 years. Do you know why the Republican Party was so weak in the South during this time? If not, you might want to conduct a Google search on the subject of the Democratic Solid South. *Provide a brief explanation on the worksheet.*

8. **Now examine the 1948 election** (Harry Truman's Democratic victory). What do you notice in the Democratic Solid South?

9. The yellow states in 1948 are states won by Strom Thurmond, a Southern Democratic Senator who became fed up with Truman's stance on race issues of the day (i.e., Truman advocated that lynching should be a federal crime, and stood for integrating the armed forces), and who therefore led a "Dixiecrat" rebellion against the Democrats. As you can see, the Solid South was beginning to rebel against the Democratic Party, and though many Southerners weren't ready to vote Republican in 1948, they were growing angry with the Democratic

Party's growing liberalism. Later, Strom Thurmond and other Southern voters would switch parties and become Republican, claiming that the Democrats had become the party of cultural liberalism, tax-and-spend welfare, and preoccupation with civil rights.

10. **Examine the 1952 and 1956 victories** of Republican Dwight Eisenhower, the war hero. Even as a Republican war hero swept the nation, how did the South vote?

11. **Examine the 1960 Kennedy victory.** Could Kennedy have won without the Democratic South?

12. In the 1960s, under Presidents Kennedy and Johnson, the Democrats became the party of Civil Rights, seeking integration and voting rights for blacks. As the 1960s wore on into the 1970s, anti-war protests and liberal movements such as feminism, environmentalism, gay rights, and welfare rights all expressed themselves through the Democratic Party. As the Democratic Party became more liberal, what happened to their "Solid South" base? **To determine the answer, examine the elections of 1964-1988.** This period includes the historic landslide victories of Republican Ronald Reagan (1980 and 1984). *Can the Democrats still define the South as their "base states" by 1988? Include the answer in the worksheet.*

13. **Examine the 1992 and 1996 elections.** In these elections, two Southern Democrats (Clinton and Gore) ran on the Democratic ticket against Republican candidates widely regarded as ineffective. The Democrats hoped that two Southerners might keep the South safe for the Democratic Party. What do these elections show in terms of which regions of the country seemed Democratic strongholds during this time: the Northeast, the South, the Midwest, the Rocky Mountain West, or the West Coast?

14. **Finally, examine the 2000 and 2004 elections** of President George W. Bush. Compare these elections to the 1996 election. You can see

which states and regions are shaping up as the modern base of the Democrats and the Republicans. *Based on these elections, use the worksheet to define five regions of the United States as either: a) Republican Base, b) Democratic Base, or c) Swing Regions. The five regions are: the Northeast, the South, the Midwest, the Rocky Mountain West, and the West Coast.*

15. In addition to classifying regions, you can be more precise and use the election maps to compile a list of individual states that can be considered "base states" or "battleground states." To do that, **use the 1996-2004 maps** to compile a scratch paper list of states that voted for the Republican presidential candidate in *all three elections* (1996, 2000 and 2004). Do the same for the Democrats. Place the remainder of states in the "battleground" or "swing state" category.

16. These lists are good starting places for 2008 Electoral College analysis, and reflect historic trends in presidential elections. But each election brings its own dynamics as different issues and changes in the values of states lead some states that were once safe to become "swing states," and vice versa. To hone your lists, and get a more accurate assessment of which states are safe for each party in 2008, and which are the current battlegrounds, you need to supplement your historic analysis with an assessment of current public opinion in each state.

17. There are many good sites for examining state-level presidential election polling data, including:

   - www.usaelectionpolls.com/2008/state-polls.html. This page has a US map. Click on any state to see a selection of recent polls.
   - www.realclearpolitics.com. Click the links for "general election polls" and "latest polls" on the right hand side of the page.
   - www.centerforpolitics.org/crystalball/2004/president. Click the link for "Sabato's Electoral Road Map" for recent analysis.
   - http://presidentpolls2008.com. Another site with a collection of presidential election polls, organized by state.

18. **Rely on at least one of these sites** to provide the analysis you need to refine your list of "safe Democratic states," "safe Republican states," and "swing states." Use the data to decide if any of your "safe" states should be moved to the "swing" category, and vice versa. You don't need to look at the data from *all* 50 states, but you should at least look at the polls in the battleground states, and examine a few of the "safe states" that you suspect might be competitive. **Examine the dynamics in about 10-15 states.** There are no undisputed criteria for how close a state has to be in the polls to be considered a "swing" state. One analyst might define a swing state as one where the candidates are separated by 3% or less in the polls. Another might choose a 5% level, while others might choose 8%. To complicate matters, there are different polls, reporting different results in terms of candidate standing in various states.

19. Use your best judgment, guided by the polls you have read, to decide which states on your original list of safe and swing states should be moved to a different category. *On the worksheet, include your final list of safe Democrat states, safe Republican states, and swing states.*

20. Now you are prepared to make your own map of "base/safe states" versus "swing/battleground states." Return to **www.270towin.com.** The default map on this page reflects a preset scenario, such as the results of the 2004 election, with all the states colored in to reflect the results of that election. But you want to begin with a neutral map, with no states colored in.

21. Use the drop-down menu at the bottom of the map to select the **"All Neutral"** view. All the states turn beige (see the screenshot on the next page).

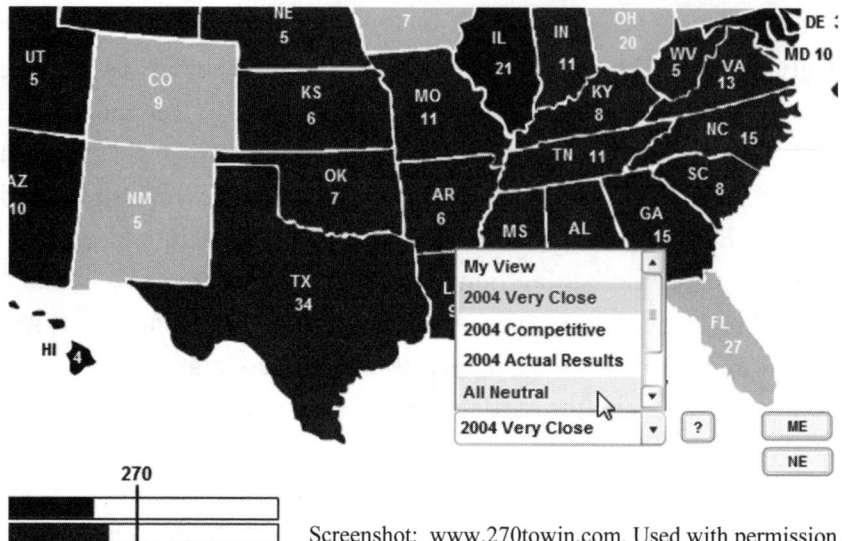

Screenshot: www.270towin.com. Used with permission.

22. Click on individual states to reflect your assessment of which states are "safe" for Democrats and Republicans and which are "battlegrounds." Click a state once to turn it red (for a "safe Republican" state), twice to turn it blue (for a "safe Democrat" state), and leave it beige to represent a "battleground" state. You can easily correct mistakes by clicking until each state is the color you desire.

23. Print your color-coded Electoral College map and turn it in with this assignment. You have created a map of the strategic considerations candidates must weigh in their race to the White House. In the next exercise, you will explore which of these battleground states to especially target in helping your candidate achieve victory.

Done!

THE ELECTORAL COLLEGE BATTLEGROUND WORKSHEET

1. What region of the country remained Democratic in the midst of the Republican presidential sweep of 1928?

2. In what region of the country did Republicans maintain strength even in the midst of the Democratic presidential sweep of 1932?

3. Briefly summarize why the South voted reliably Democratic from the 1870s to the 1970s.

4. Describe the South's voting patterns between 1964 and 1988: Was the South generally Democratic, generally Republican, or generally mixed?

5. Based on the elections of 1996-2004, place five American regions (Northeast, South, Midwest, Rocky Mountain West, and West Coast) in the categories below.

    A) Democratic Base Region:

    B) Republican Base Region:

    C) Swing Region:

6. Provide your final list of Safe and Swing States described in step 19.

Safe Republican States	Safe Democratic States	Battleground States

7. Did any states shift places from where you originally placed them in step 15? If so, describe your reasoning for moving at least one state.

8. Print your Electoral College map and attach it to this worksheet

ISSUE SIX:
TARGETING THE BATTLEGROUND STATES

In this exercise, you will continue your work in the previous exercise as a mock campaign consultant to one of the major political parties. In the previous exercise, you defined and mapped "safe states" and "battleground states." Though you now know where all the battleground states are, it is unlikely that your chosen candidate has the resources to focus on all battleground states equally. Your candidate needs to decide which battleground states offer the best chance for victory, and focus resources there. Your task is to determine which set of battleground states your chosen candidate should focus on, in order to win at least 270 Electoral College votes.

1. First, choose a party to design a winning strategy for.

2. To examine what possible "Winning Combinations" of battleground states exist for your party in the scenario you built in the previous exercise, return to **www.270towin.com**. Repeat steps 22-23 in the previous exercise to rebuild the map you created there.

3. Once you have rebuilt the map, the "Road to 270" tool at the bottom of the webpage provides updates. An example of the tool is in the screenshot below, showing that the tool has several functions:

   - In the "Votes" column, it updates how many electoral votes are safe for each party in your scenario.

   - In the "Remaining" column, it updates how many "Remaining" electoral votes are needed by each party to win.

- In the "Must Win" column, it updates which (if any) of the remaining battleground states MUST be won by one or the other party in your scenario in order to win the presidency.

- You can click on the "**Winning Combinations**" link to the far right of this tool's window to see *all* possible combinations of battleground states that will give one or the other party the presidency in your scenario.

The Road to 270

	Votes	Remaining	Must Win	
🐴 Democrats	252	18	–	9 Winning Combinations »
🐘 Republicans	203	67	FL,OH	8 Winning Combinations »

When 12 or fewer states remain undecided on the 2008 map, you will see the number of possible combinations remaining to get each party's candidate to 270 Electoral Votes. Click the link provided to see each winning combination.

Screenshot: www.270towin.com. Used with permission.

4. *Create a list of ALL battleground states that exist in your scenario, as you will use this list in later steps. List up to eight of these battleground states on the worksheet.* Now click on the "**Winning Combinations**" link, described in step 3. These combinations are examples of various MINIMAL combinations of your battleground states that will lead to victory (assuming your candidate also wins all the safe states that you came up with in the previous exercise). Your party may, of course, seek to win more states than the minimum necessary to win the election. But for this exercise you will come up with a *minimal* combination of battleground states that, if won, would be enough to give your party the presidency. Focusing on just enough states to win allows your party to target resources wisely and not spread them too thinly.

*Print these various combinations for your later reference, as you will return to these winning combinations in step 22. You should now have two lists: one with **all** battleground states, and one with **minimal winning combinations** of battleground states.*

5. Your choice of which minimal combination of swing states to pursue cannot be random. You need to determine which of these states your

party has the best chance in. You can't simply rely on polling data to tell you what state to focus on, since you've already used polling data to determine that the state is, indeed, up for grabs.

6. There are many strategies in addition to polls for determining which are truly the most promising of swing states. One strategy is to examine the demographics of the swing states (for example, the race/ethnicity, church-going habits, and income level of residents), in hopes of finding which state has the kind of demographics that might bias the state in your favor. For example, history shows that Latino and Black voters strongly favor the Democratic Party. Does the data show that some battleground states have a high percentage of Black and Latino voters? If so, perhaps those battleground states should be targeted by Democrats. On the other hand, historic data indicates that people who attend church regularly are far more likely to vote Republican. So perhaps Republicans should target battleground states with a high percentage of regular church goers.

7. You already know the possible combinations of winning states that exist for your party (step 4, above). Now you need to determine what demographics are favorable to your party, and then find which of the winning combinations of states has a good mix of those demographics. To determine what kind of voter groups (i.e., demographics) are favorable to your party, go to **www.cnn.com/ELECTION/2004/ pages/results/states/US/P/00/epolls.0.html**.

8. Here you find the CNN exit polling data from the 2004 election. Based on this data, you can determine which groups tended to vote for Bush and which tended to vote for Kerry. For example, in the screenshot on the next page you learn that white voters (especially white men) were far more likely than non-whites to vote for the Republican candidate.

VOTE BY GENDER

	BUSH		KERRY
TOTAL	**2004**	**2000**	**2004**
Male (46%)	55%	+2	44%
Female (54%)	48%	+5	51%

Screenshot: www.cnn.com

VOTE BY RACE AND GENDER

	BUSH		KERRY
TOTAL	**2004**	**2000**	**2004**
White Men (36%)	62%	n/a	37%
White Women (41%)	55%	n/a	44%
Non-White Men (10%)	30%	n/a	67%
Non-White Women (12%)	24%	n/a	75%

9. Scroll through the exit polling data on this site. You can see that about the first quarter of questions relate *demographic data to voting patterns* (e.g., education and income levels, race and gender, church attendance and union membership). Many of the questions in the later parts of the survey address *voter sentiments, rather than demographics* (liberal versus conservative ideology, voter opinions on Iraq and the economy, etc.). At the very end, additional demographic questions appear (i.e., vote by size of the community). You are most interested in the demographic questions, so that you can determine which kinds of demographics (e.g., churchgoers? Non-whites? Rural voters?) are more likely to support your party's candidate.

10. Pick two or three key demographic variables that seem to clearly divide the electorate between the two candidates, *and* that you predict are likely to vary by state (see example in screenshot on next page).

VOTE BY INCOME

Screenshot: www.cnn.com

> Union households are generally pro-Democrat. You can predict that some states have more union households that others.

	2004	2000	2004
	49%	n/a	50%
	58%	n/a	41%

ANYONE IN HOUSEHOLD IN A UNION?

		BUSH		KERRY
TOTAL	2004	2000	2004
Yes (24%)	40%	n/a	59%
No (76%)	55%	n/a	44%

11. *On the worksheet, list the variables you chose and describe how each variable influences the vote for your party's candidate (for example, you could say: "the more union households, the fewer GOP votes").*

12. Now that you have the key demographics, you need to determine which swing states are the most promising for your candidate on these variables. For example, if you are working for the Democrats, and you choose union households as a favorable variable, you now need to determine which swing states have numerous union households.

13. Begin by reviewing the battleground state analysis at CNN's election center at **http://edition.cnn.com/ELECTION/2008/**. In the menu at the top of the page, you can learn more about battleground states by clicking on the link for **"States to Watch"** (at the top of the page).

Meet the Candidates

Screenshot: www.cnn.com

14. A list of profiled battleground states appears. If you see some of your battleground states, click on them for a host of information, including recent polls, historic voting patterns, demographics and video clips.

Review the data, keeping in mind what you already know about the kinds of demographics that are favorable to your candidate. For each of your possible battleground states, find at least one good reason why your candidate should or should not focus on that state. It might be a demographic reason, or it might be different reason such as the historic voting trends in the state. Include the reason on the worksheet.

15. The CNN website may not have the kind of demographic data you identified as critical in step 10, above. For additional demographic data, there are several websites where you can gain state-level information. Steps 16–23, below, provide possible sources to find your information, **but you don't have to follow each of these steps**. You just want to follow the steps that seem most likely to lead you to the kind of demographic information you have decided to focus on (see brief guide below).

- Steps 16–20 describe two broad data sets on a variety of demographic data (e.g., race, income, marriage, and labor data).

- Step 21 describes data on Hispanic percentage, by state.

- Step 22 describes data on church attendance patterns, by state.

- Step 23 describes data on gun ownership rates, by state.

- If you need data that you can't find in these steps, conduct an Internet search.

16. One good site for demographic data is the Kaiser Family Foundation's "State Health Facts" site. Access it at **www.statehealthfacts.org**. Once there, you can click on **"50 State Comparisons"** or

"Demographics and the Economy" to pull up a list of demographics on which to compare the 50 states, including such factors as race and ethnicity, age, number of union employees and income.

Screenshot: www.statehealthfacts.org. The Henry J. Kaiser Family Foundation, 2008.

17. One of the most complete sources for a variety of demographic data is the Census Bureau's American FactFinder website. Here you can get the most updated Census estimates about the people of the United States. To use it, go to: **http://factfinder.census.gov**.

18. The screenshot on the next page appears. You are interested in updated census estimates based on the most recent surveys (not the old data from the 2000 census), so click the link to **"Get Data"** from the American Community Survey. The American Community Survey reports Census Bureau estimates of the most current demographic data from the various states, based on polling that the Census Bureau conducts on a regular basis nationwide.

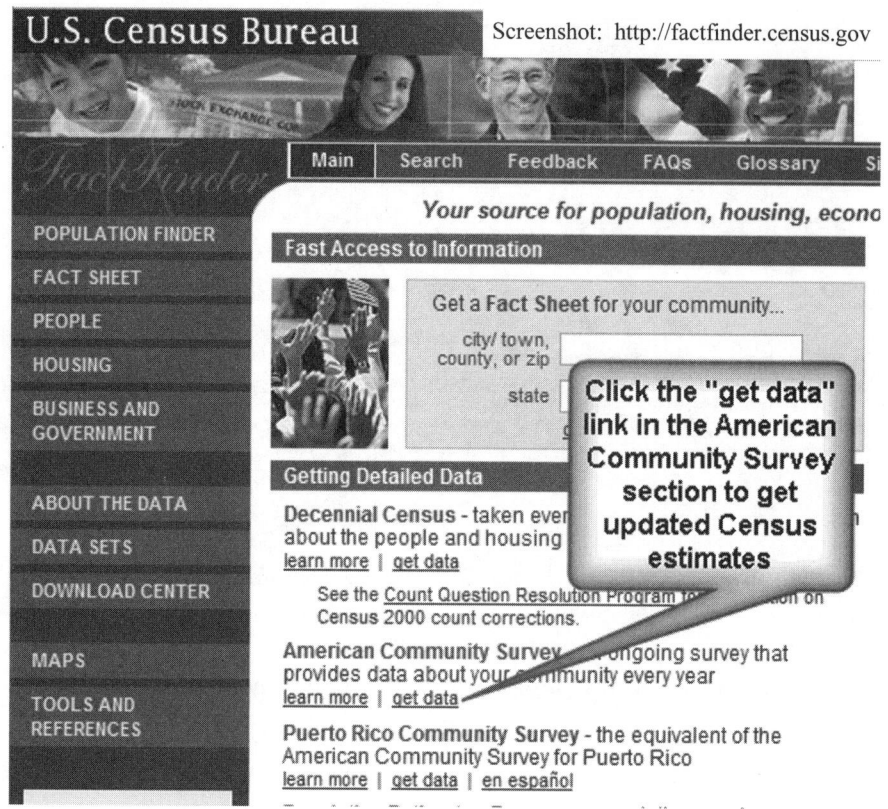

Screenshot: http://factfinder.census.gov

19. When the next screen appears, select the button for the **"2006 American Community Survey,"** and select the **"Ranking Tables"** option from the menu to the left (see screenshot below).

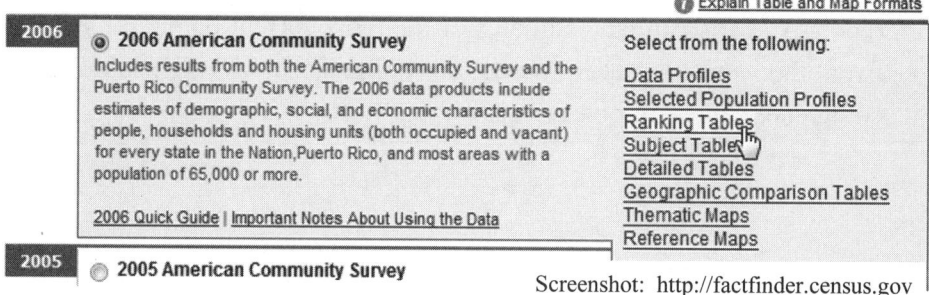

Screenshot: http://factfinder.census.gov

20. A list of tables appears. Click on any variable and the state rankings appear. For example, you could click on "Percent of Households that are Married Couple Families," (a variable that CNN exit polls suggest

is meaningful in predicting presidential votes) and the state rankings pop up. Perhaps, if you are working for the Republicans, your Party should target the swing states with high levels of married families.

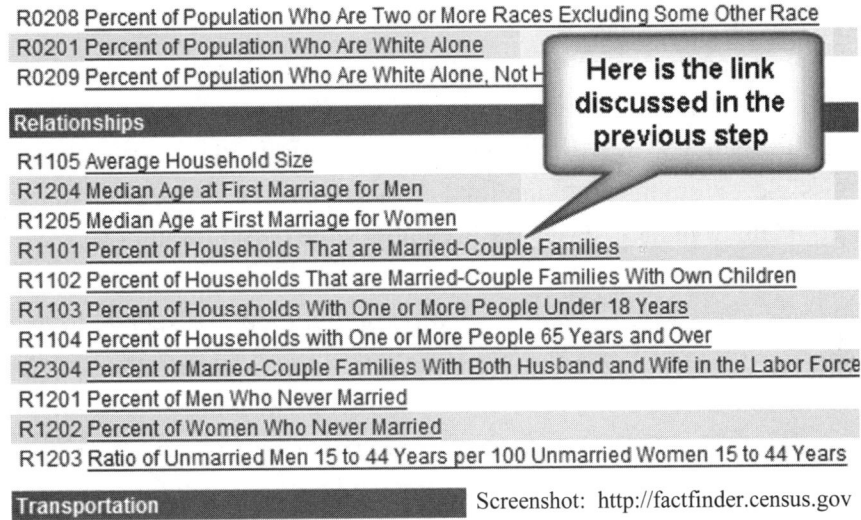

Screenshot: http://factfinder.census.gov

21. To view the percent of Hispanic residents by state, go to the Pew Center's report at **http://pewhispanic.org/reports/middecade/**. Once there, scroll down and select the link to "**Table 10: Hispanic Population by State, 2000 and 2005.**" You can even assess in which states Hispanics are growing fastest, which might be useful in deciding which swing states to target or avoid for your party of choice.

22. If you are interested in church attendance patterns by state, you can read a San Diego Union-Tribune article at this website: www.signonsandiego.com/uniontrib/20060502/news_1z1n2thelist.html.

23. If you are interested in learning the percent of all households in various states that own a gun (a statistic that CNN exit polls suggest is related to election voting patterns), you can visit this website: **www.schs.state.nc.us/SCHS/brfss/2001/us/firearm3.html**.

24. Based on these data sources, or others that you discover on your own, you can determine which of the battleground states has demographics most favorable to the party of your candidate.

25. Return to the list of all possible "winning combinations" of battleground states that you printed in step 4. Review the possible winning combinations that exist for your party, and compare them to all the data you have gathered on the various states. Which of the possible winning combinations looks like the best one for your candidate to pursue, based on favorable state demographics?

26. *On the worksheet, list the "winning combination" of swing states that you have decided are best for your party/candidate (there is room to list up to 6 states on the worksheet, so if your winning combination has more than six states, just list your top six states). Briefly describe your reasoning for why each of those states should be specifically targeted by the party you have chosen to consult for.* You have just crafted an intelligent strategy for winning the Electoral College.

Done!

TARGETING BATTLEGROUND STATES

1. What party/candidate did you choose to consult for?

2. List two or three demographic variables and describe how each variable relates to the vote for your chosen party/candidate.

3. Fill in the chart below with up to eight key battleground states.

Swing State	A reason your party should or should not focus here

4. List all the states in the winning combination of battleground states that you ended up with (but no more than 6 states). Describe why the dynamics in each state are favorable to your candidate. In some cases, a state may not have favorable dynamics, but may be a state that your party has to win nonetheless, to make the "winning combination" work. Note all states that fall into that category.

"Must Win" Swing State	Why this State Is Favorable

Presidential elections involve more than just the headliner election between the two major candidates. Together with a president, America elects one-third of its Senators and all 435 members of the House of Representatives in presidential election years. These congressional elections are very important to the presidential candidates (winning candidates want to govern with their party in control of Congress), and the congressional elections are often heavily influenced by developments in the presidential election (such as the popularity of the sitting president, the popularity of the presidential candidates, and national economic conditions).

When a winning presidential candidate proves so popular that his victory helps congressional candidates of the president's party win their own races, we call this the "coattail effect"—congressional candidates ride into office sitting on the president's long coattails. It can work the other way too. Sometimes presidential candidates are so unpopular that when they lose, many congressional candidates of the president's party also lose, caught up in the national rejection of the president's party. Something like this happened in the election of 1980, when Carter proved such an unpopular presidential candidate (against Reagan), that his party lost numerous congressional seats, turning control of the Senate over to the Republicans.

Though some congressional elections are very responsive to national dynamics, such as the presidential election and economic conditions, many others are insulated from such dynamics, and are known as "safe seats," in which the winning party can be predicted years in advance and which can hardly ever be affected by such things as presidential coattails. These are districts like liberal San Francisco, which always elects Democrats to the House, and conservative Utah which always sends a Republican Senator to Congress, no matter what is going on in the presidential election. Or they are districts held by popular incumbents that no challenger can hope to upset, such as Ted Kennedy of Massachusetts.

For a variety of reasons, most congressional seats are considered "safe" every year and only a minority of races are categorized as "swing seats"— congressional races that are contestable and that could go to either party. It is the swing seats that hold the fate to control of Congress. It is these swing seats that you will focus on in this exercise, as you seek to become a swing seat forecaster, predicting the outcome of key congressional races in the 2008 election, based partly upon dynamics at the presidential level.

Election results for the swing seats are determined by a variety of factors, including the nature of the local race itself (e.g., the quality of the local candidates and local events that shake up a race). Swing seat races are also often affected by broader national dynamics. Scholars have shown that key broader indicators affecting (or at least predicting) local races include the popularity within the district of the sitting president, the breakdown of the presidential vote in the district, and the state of the economy in the area, especially unemployment and personal income levels.[1]

In this exercise, you will categorize five key Senate races and eight key House races as "swing seats." You will apply a variety of indicators to each race (such as party strength in the district, local presidential popularity, and state economic trends). In the end, you will make predictions for each race, which you can look back on after the election to evaluate your skills as an elections pundit.

---

[1] J.E. Campbell. "Predicting Seat Gains from Presidential Coattails." *American Journal of Political Science* 30 (1986): 165-183;   A. I. Abramowitz. "Economic Conditions, Presidential Popularity, and Voting Behavior in Midterm Congressional Elections." *The Journal of Politics* 47 (1985): 31-43;   J. Beatty. "The 'S' Word Spells Trouble for the GOP." *The Atlantic.com* (August 15, 2006), www.theatlantic.com/doc/200608u/stagflation (accessed on November 24, 2007).

PREDICTING THE SWING SEATS

1. Begin by exploring the kinds of national variables scholars use to predict overall gains or losses of House of Representative Seats for the political parties in any given election. For a very basic look at this prediction process, you can pull up an online web tool that quickly allows you to predict overall Democratic and Republican gains/losses in the House of Representatives based on national indicators. Go to **http://adambrown.info/p/tools/house**.

2. The "House Elections Predictor" tool of Adam Brown, a California political scientist, opens. The tool is easy to use. You can see that there are four key national variables used to predict the overall change in the House of Representatives in the 2008 election: the presidential approval rating, real income growth, the number of House seats held by the President's party, and the average number of House seats held by Republicans over the last 16 years. These variables are already pre-set with relatively current data, but you can update or change the variables as you wish (for example, you could input a higher or lower presidential approval rating). When you are done editing the variables, click the "predict the outcome" button at the bottom of the page. *Write your prediction on the worksheet so that after the election you can reflect on the usefulness of this national-level tool.*

3. In the rest of this exercise, you will complete district-level predictions of individual swing-seat results. This process is different from simply examining overall national economic conditions and national presidential popularity, which can allow an observer to predict the *overall* number of seats that will be gained or lost in Congress by the two parties, *but which cannot predict any specific race.*

4. To begin, you will need to determine five closely contested Senate seats and eight closely contested House seats on which to focus. Closely contested seats are called the "swing seats," as they could swing either

way. Seats are considered "swing seats" due to a variety of factors, such as the absence of an incumbent running for the seat and public opinion polls that show the election for the seat to be very close.

5. To come up with your list of contestable swing seats, begin by visiting the website of "Sabato's Crystal Ball." This site of the University of Virginia's Center for Politics is where the research team of political scientist Larry Sabato provides their electoral analysis and predictions. Go to **www.centerforpolitics.org/crystalball**.

6. There is interesting political analysis throughout this website. Explore any of it you like. When you are ready, click the **"Senate"** link under the **"2008"** section on the left side of the website, as in the screenshot.

Screenshot: www.centerforpolitics.org. Used with permission.

7. You are taken to a map of the United States, with each state color-coded to represent whether the contested Senate seat is currently held by a Republican (red) or by a Democrat (blue). If a state is colored grey, it means the state has no Senate election in 2008. You can see that most of the 33 open Senate seats are currently held by Republicans (21), and only 12 are held by Democrats. This is known as a high degree of Republican "exposure," and suggests that Republican risk in this election is much greater than Democratic risk.

Screenshot: www.centerforpolitics.org. Used with permission.

8. To get information about the Senate race in any specific state, click on that state. Professor Sabato's analysis pops up. He classifies the states as "Strong" for the Democrats or the Republicans, "Leaning" towards one or the other party, or as "Tossups." Spend some time calling up various state races, or click the **"View All Races"** link to the bottom left of the map, and you can see analysis of all open Senate races.

9. Based on your review of this data, come up with a list of 5-7 Senate races that are either "tossups" or "leaners" that you think deserve further attention as "swing seat" races. Jot these races down on a separate sheet of paper because you will need them in a later step. **Don't add these races to the exercise worksheet yet.**

10. Click the **"House"** option under the **"2008"** menu section to the left of the website. Professor Sabato's analysis of closely contested House seats pops us. The website also includes important facts such as recent polling data and the percent of the vote in 2006 that was received by each of the vulnerable candidates (see screenshot on next page).

A Look Ahead at Potentially Vulnerable House Seats in 2008

Democrats Below 55 Percent of the Two-P

Member	State	District	Vote Percentage
Joe Courtney	CT	02	50.02
John Barrow	GA	12	50.30
Patrick Murphy	PA	08	50.30
Jim Marshall	GA	08	50.55
Tim Mahoney	FL	16	50.97
Steve Kagen	WI	08	51.07

Screenshot: www.centerforpolitics.org. Used with permission.

11. Examine the data, and come up with a list of 10-15 key House seats that might be considered "swing seats" in the 2008 election. Jot these seats down on a separate sheet of paper, with simple notations such as "NY19" and "PA08" to represent "New York's 19th Congressional District" and "Pennsylvania's 8th." **Don't add these races to your final exercise worksheet yet.**

12. You have come up with a rough draft of swing seats on which to focus. To finalize your list, you will examine the analysis at one other website, the "Cook Political Report." Go to **http://cookpolitical.com/**.

13. Explore the interesting political analysis on this website. When you are ready, click the **"Senate Races"** button on the left side of the website. Then click the **"Senate Race Ratings"** link in the list that appears.

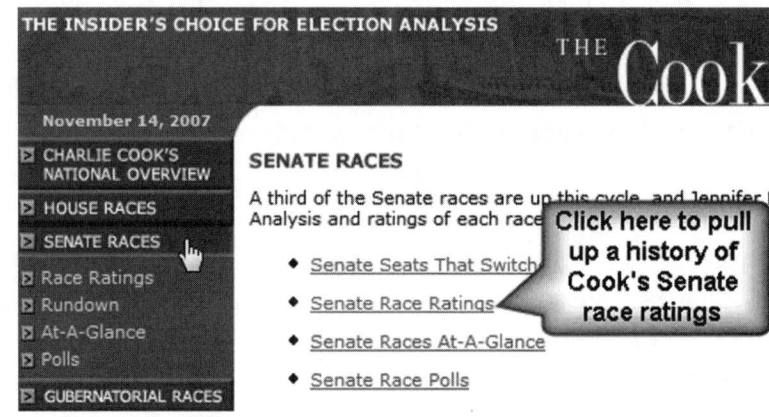

Screenshot: http://www.cookpolitical.com. Used with permission.

14. A list of the Cook Report's Senate **"Race Ratings"** appears, going back to 2006 and beyond. You only need to look at the most recent ratings sheet available (the one at the top of the list). Click that link.

Screenshot: http://cookpolitical.com. Used with permission.

15. A spreadsheet pops up with analysis of which Senate seats are "Solid" and which are "Likely" for each party. You can also see which races are merely "Leaning" toward a party, and which are true "Tossups." As you can see in the screenshot below, taken at the end of October 2007, there were only six Senate seats considered truly contestable by the Cook report at that time (5 of them held by Republicans). Things may change by the time you view the latest Cook analysis.

Lean: These are considered competitive races but one party has an advantage.
Toss-Up: These are the most competitive races; either party has a good chance of

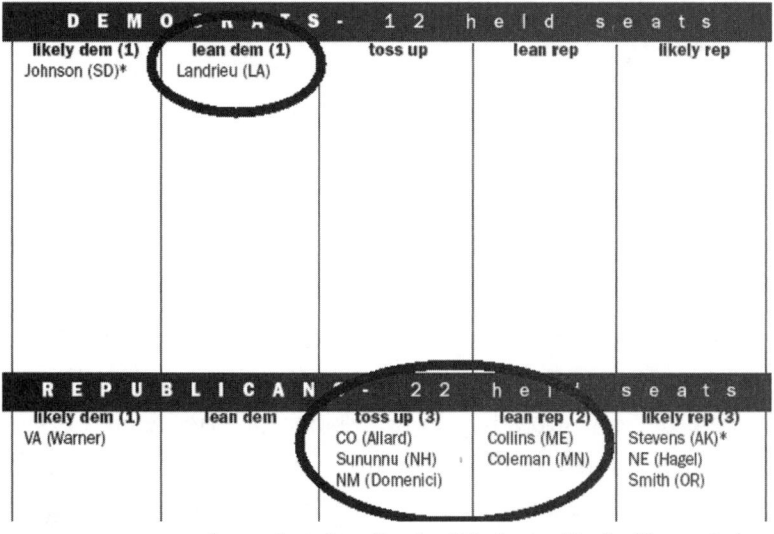

Screenshot: http://cookpolitical.com. Used with permission.

16. Now that you have reviewed the analysis from both the Sabato and Cook websites, you can hone your own list of five contestable, swing Senate seats. You may have to chose some seats from the "likely Dem" or "likely Republican" columns to come up with five Senate seats, depending on political dynamics when you complete this exercise. By comparing the analysis you learned at both sites, come up with the five Senate seats you think are the most contestable. *Fill in those races in the first five slots in the attached worksheet, using an abbreviation such as "CO-Sen" to indicate the Colorado Senate race.*

17. Return to the Cook Report's main page and click the **"House Races"** menu to the left of the screen. Now click the **"Competitive Race Chart"** option, as shown in the screen shot below.

Screenshot: http://cookpolitical.com. Used with permission.

18. Click the most recent **"House Competitive Race Chart"** that appears.

19. The chart on the next page appears, with a list of seats that this website considers tossups, and a list of seats that are "Leaning" or "Likely" for the Democratic or Republican parties. The page also has a "PVI" number for each district. The Partisan Voter Index (PVI) number is a measure of how strongly a congressional district leans to one party or the other, compared to the nation as a whole. It is computed by averaging the presidential election votes in a district for the last two elections and comparing them to the national election results (for

example, a PVI of R+2 would mean the district vote for the Republican presidential candidate in the last two elections averaged 2 percentage points higher than the national vote for the Democratic candidates).

LIKELY DEMOCRATIC			LEAN DEMOCRATIC		

The "PVI" is the "Partisan Voter Index." It is the measure of how much the congressional district's votes in the last two presidential elections varied from the national vote, in terms of being more Democratic or Republican. A PVI of D+8 means that Democratic presidential candidates in the last two elections averaged 8% better in this congressional district than they did in the nation as a whole.

DISTRICT	REPRESENTATIVE	PVI	DISTRICT	REPRESENTATIVE	PVI
CT-02	Joe Courtney	D+8			
CT-05	Chris Murphy	D+4	AZ-05	Harry Mitchell	R+4
GA-12	John Barrow	D+2	AZ-08	Gabrielle Giffords	R+1
IL-08	Melissa Bean	R+5	CA-11	Jerry McNerney	R+3
IN-02	Joe Donnelly	R+4	FL-16	Tim Mahoney	R+2
IN-07	VACANT(Carson)	D+9			

Screenshot: http://cookpolitical.com. Used with permission.

20. Use this chart, plus the material you learned from Sabato's Crystal Ball site, to finalize your list of eight contestable "swing seats" in the House of Representatives. You can use the PVI index to help guide you, since it is a measure of how strongly each of the districts tilts toward the Democrats or Republicans compared to the nation as a whole. *Fill in your final eight House swing seats in the first column on the attached worksheet, using notations such as "AZ-08" to represent "Arizona's 8th Congressional District." Also include the PVI index in the worksheet. You will use the PVI index in a later step.*

21. Now that you have a list of five Senate races and eight House races on which to focus, you need a strategy to come up with predictions of the ultimate winner. You can't simply rely on opinion polls, since these races were defined as "contestable" by virtue of the fact that the polls are close. If the most recent polling data shows a candidate easily pulling away, then maybe polls alone will be enough to rely on, but this exercise will also use additional tools for predicting a congressional race.

22. Important variables effecting a congressional race include: a) the underlying party composition of the district (is it generally a Republican or Democratic district?), b) the popularity of the president (a popular president will help congressional candidates of his party, and an unpopular one will hurt them), and c) economic conditions in the district (for example, unemployment levels and the rate at which personal income is growing).

23. Your worksheet has room for filling in all these variables for each of your 15 swing seat candidates. Let's begin with underlying party strength in each of your chosen districts.

24. For the House candidates, this data is at your fingertips already. You should have already filled in the PVI index for each of your House seats in step 20. If you didn't, do so now. This PVI index is a measure of how well the Republican and Democratic candidates for president did in this district in the previous two elections, as compared to national results. You can use it as a measure of underlying Republican or Democratic strength in the district. The higher the PVI number, the bigger the advantage to whichever party is listed in the PVI index, which arguably tilts the district in favor of that same party winning this contestable seat in 2008.

25. For this exercise, you will devise a revised version of a "PVI" score for each *Senate* seat. You will give each Senate seat a score based on the winning presidential candidate's margin of victory in that state in

2004. This is not the same as the Cook Report's PVI scores for House Seats, but it will provide an estimate of party strength in contested Senate races. To determine the Senate figures, you need to know the statewide vote for president in 2004 for each of your five chosen seats (because people vote for Senators on a statewide basis). If one of your states voted for Kerry by a 53% to 47% margin, you would give that state a "PVI" score of D+6 (indicating that the Democrats beat the Republicans by 6% in this state, determined by subtracting the Republican presidential vote percentage from the Democratic percentage in the state).

26. To find the statewide vote for president in 2004, go to **www.cnn.com/ELECTION/2004/pages/results/president/.** Click on any state you like to get the popular percentage for each presidential candidate.

27. *Determine the Party presidential vote advantage for each of the Senate races you have chosen to focus on. Remember that this presidential vote advantage number for the Senate seats will be determined by figuring out the percent by which one party beat the other in the presidential race: for example, a 55% to 45% Republican victory in a state would be a "R+10" PVI (because 55 minus 45 is 10). Fill in those numbers under the PVI column on the worksheet.*

28. The next variable you will focus on is the president's current approval rating in the states that are hosting the various elections you are focusing on. Since the current president is a Republican, exceptionally high or low approval ratings can be expected to affect congressional Republican candidates, either pro or con. There is no magic number at which the president's approval rating definitely helps or hurts, but you can generally say that state approval ratings well below the national average are probably bad news for state-level candidates of the president's party, and state approval ratings above the national average may suggest Republican strength in that state.

29. You can find state-by-state presidential approval ratings at **www.presidentpolls2008.com**. Click "Bush approval ratings by state" to the left of the website (see screenshot on the next page). Find recent approval ratings for each of the states in which you have a targeted election. *Fill the information in your worksheet.*

Screenshot: www.presidentpolls2008.com. Used with permission.

30. Finally, you need to find state-by-state economic data, so you can determine if your targeted seats are in states that are suffering or succeeding economically: is the unemployment rate going up or down in each state? Is personal income growing faster or slower than the rest of the nation? If economic conditions look good in the state, it's good news for Republican candidates, since the party of the sitting president is often rewarded by the voters for good economic conditions and punished for poor ones.

31. Begin by examining unemployment trends in your targeted states. Go to **www.bls.gov/lau**. This is the website for the Bureau of Labor Statistics, which has the data you need.

32. Click the link titled **"Tables and Maps created by BLS"** (see screenshot on the next page).

U.S. Department of Labor
Bureau of Labor Statistics

Local Area Unemployment Statistics

www.bls.gov

BLS Home | Programs & Surveys | Get Detailed Statistics | Glossary | What's New | Find

The **Local Area Unemployment Statistics (L**...d ?
unemployment, and labor force data for Cer...ou
areas, and many cities, by place of residenc

Click here for state-level unemployment data

- General Overview
- Economic News Releases
- Special Notices
- Get Detailed LAUS Statistics
- Tables and Maps Created by BLS
- Publications and Other Documentation
- Related Links

33. Now click on the link for **"Over-the-Year Change in Unemployment Rates for States."** See screenshot below.

TABLES AND MAPS CREATED BY BLS:

Monthly

Regional and State Employment and Unemployment (Monthly)

Supplemental Tables

Here is the annual unemployment data that you need

- Current Unemployment Rates for States and Historical ...ghs/Lows
- Unemployment Rates for States
- Over-the-Month Change in Unemployment Rates fo...States
- Over-the-Year Change in Unemployment Rates for States
- Employment Status of the Civilian Noninstitutional Population by State NEW

Supplemental Map

- Unemployment rates by state, seasonally adjusted (GIF)
- Unemployment rates by state, seasonally adjusted (PDF)

Metropolitan Area Employment and Unemployment (M... Screenshot: www.bls.gov

34. A table appears with the most recent data. You are interested in the figure in the "Change" column of this chart (the last column). That column shows how much unemployment has changed, up or down, for each state in the last year. *Find the figure for each of your targeted states and add it to your worksheet.* Any state with a high positive

number has experienced significantly growing unemployment, which is a bad sign for Republican candidates. A negative number means unemployment is shrinking, which may be good for Republican candidates in that state.

35. Your last piece of data is personal income figures: is personal income in your targeted states growing quickly or not?

   Go to **www.bea.gov/regional/index.htm#state**. This is the webpage for the Bureau of Economic Analysis, and they have annual reports on personal income growth in each state.

36. Scroll down to the **"State Annual Personal Income"** link, as seen in the screen shot below.

Regional Economic Accounts

Gross Domestic Product (GDP) by State and Metropolitan Area

State annual estimates
▸ News Release: Gross Domestic Product by State
   †includes highlights and associated tables

📊 Interactive Tables: Gross Domestic Product by State

⬤ Interactive Maps: Gross Domestic Product by State Interactive Map

▸ Gross Domestic Product by State Estimation Methodology

Metropolitan area annual estimates
▸ News Release: Gross Domestic Product by Metropolitan Area
   †includes highlights and associated tables

📊 Interactive Tables: Gross Domestic Product

> Click here for state-level personal income data

State and Local Area Personal Income

⬤ Interactive Maps: Regional Economic Measurement Division (REMD) Interactive Map

State quarterly income estimates
▸ News Release: State Personal Income
   †includes highlights and associated tables

▸ Disaster adjustments in state personal income

Screenshot: www.bea.gov

37. A webpage appears that allows you to find the recent personal income growth rate in each of your targeted states. On the top of this page there should be a map that compares income growth in the various states (see step 38 if there is no map). *Examine this map, and fill in your worksheet by noting whether each of your targeted states is in the bottom two ranges, the middle/average range, or in the top two ranges of income growth, compared to other states.*

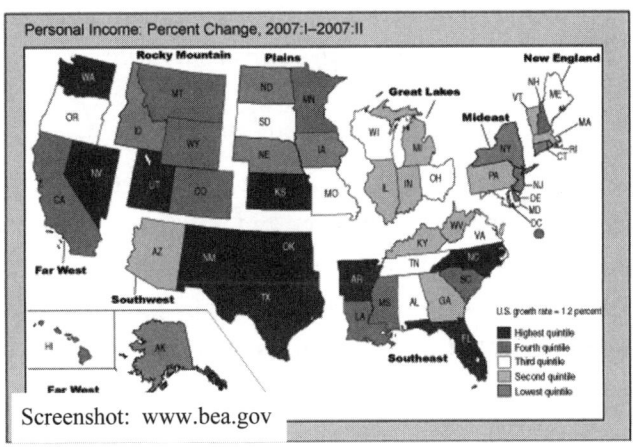

Screenshot: www.bea.gov

38. **Skip this step if you completed the previous step.** If the map is not present in step 37, there will be a spreadsheet lower down the page with a column called "Rank." That column will show where each of your targeted states is ranked, compared to the other 50 states, in terms of income growth. This data will also allow you to note whether each of your states is in the bottom group of states (states ranked 35-50), is average (states ranked 16-34), or is in the top group of states (states ranked 1-15) in terms of income growth. *Based either on the map or on the chart, fill in the information in your worksheet.*

and Region, 2006:I-2007:II								
ıl rate]		[Seasonally change from preceing quarter/1]						Rank
		Percent change from preceding quarter/1						
:I/r	2007:II/p	2006:II	2006:III	2006:IV	2007:I	2007:II	2007:I-2007:II	
3,768	11,595,412	1.2	1.0	1.5	2.5	1.2	--	
7,829	188,663	0.3	0.6	1.7	3.8	0.4	48	
3,705	44,240	1.7	0.6	0.7	2.3	1.2	29	
1,282	314,829	1.3	0.5	2.0	2.4	1.1	35	
3,797	54,518	0.9	0.6	3.3	0.2	1.3	19	
1,584	41,802	2.0	1.4	0.8	2.7	0.5	47	
				0.8	2.2	1.1	33	

Screenshot: www.bea.gov

39. Now you have a worksheet with 13 targeted "swing seats," or competitive races. Polls alone aren't enough to predict the outcomes of these races, because the polls are close. For each race, you have a set of other indicators, including the "Presidential Vote Index" in the district, the president's popularity in that state, and two important economic indicators. Based on this data, plus whatever other insight you may have gained in researching these races, make a prediction for the ultimate victor (Democrat or Republican) in each of these swing seats. *Fill in your worksheet with your predictions.*

Although scholars have sophisticated scientific formulas with which to analyze all these variables in making their election predictions, you can simply rely on your intuition and logic after reviewing the data you have come up with. Below is a sample line from a possible worksheet to help you envision how your completed worksheet will look. The numbers below are invented sample numbers—NOT the real numbers from Colorado.

Five Contested Senate Races	PVI: Partisan Voter Index	Presidential Approval Rate in State	Unemploy- ment Rate Change in Previous Year	Personal Income Ranking of State in Rate of Growth	Predicted Winner: Rep (R) or Dem (D)?
Colorado	R+2	38%	+2	Low (35th)	D

Done, and good luck!

You have created your own "Crystal Ball" for election predictions. You can return your prediction sheet after the election to see how close your predictions were to the actual results.

PREDICTING SWING SEAT WORKSHEET

What Prediction did you end up with by using Adam's House
Election Predictor Tool (step 2 of the exercise)?

Include Information for Senate and House swing seats in charts below

Five Contested Senate Races	Presidential Vote Advantage in State in 2004 (steps 25-27)	Presidential Approval Rating in State	Unemploy-ment Rate Change in Previous Year	State Personal Income Ranking: Lowest Tier, Average, or Highest Tier	Predicted Winner: Dem or Rep?

Eight Contested House Races	Presidential Vote Advantage in State in 2004 (steps 25-27)	Presidential Approval Rating in State	State Unemployment Rate Change in Previous Year	Personal Income Ranking of State: Lowest Tier, Average, or Highest Tier	Predicted Winner: Dem or Rep?

"That was really the end of my campaign that night." This is how Democratic candidate Walter Mondale remembers the importance of his 1984 presidential debate with Ronald Reagan—a debate in which Reagan charmed the audience with humorous remarks about his age.[1] In their potential for drama and unpredictability, and in the amount of press coverage surrounding them, there are few events in a presidential election that can compete with the debates. Face-to-face debates between the major political candidates have become some of the most anticipated, most viewed, and most significant events of the election season.

A candidate's performance in a debate can make the difference between winning and losing. The first presidential debates were the famous 1960 debates between Kennedy and Nixon. Most analysts conclude that Nixon looked pale, anxious and in ill-health on the television next to the tanned, confident and rested Kennedy—and that this appearance had a lot to do with Nixon losing the election. Ronald Reagan's famous one-liner during his 1976 debate with Jimmy Carter ("There you go again") is remembered as playing a role in his election victory. Bill Clinton's warm connection with voters in the 1992 "Town Hall" debates (where individual voters ask questions) is credited with having helped him to beat George H. W. Bush.

Many voters watch the debates closely, allowing candidates a unique opportunity for serious communication with the voters. Scholars Kathleen H. Jamieson and David Birdsell call the debates "serious, ad-free, sustained encounters" that encourage voters to engage in serious conversations with each other about what they saw and heard.[2] Debates also place candidates in a less predictable and less scripted environment than usual. As Jamieson and Birdsell note, "a phalanx of consultants and advisers can [usually] hide a candidate behind carefully scripted and staged speeches and professionally produced ads"—but this doesn't work in a debate, where voters can judge the character of a candidate by how he or she responds to an unpredictable confrontation with an opponent.[3]

Not everyone agrees with the potential of debates to educate voters. Richard Nixon, remembering how his 1960 defeat was partly due to Kennedy's charming appearance on television, concluded the following: "As for television debates in general, I doubt that they can ever serve a responsible role in defining the issues of a presidential campaign. Because of the nature of the medium, there will inevitably be a greater premium on showmanship than on statesmanship."[4] Many observers share Nixon's concern that the debates are mostly about style, image and silly one-liners, rather than about substance.

In this exercise, you will explore whether the debates help to create an informed electorate. You will view video clips from historic presidential debates. You will learn from these clips what to look for in this year's debate. In the end, the exercise will help you answer important questions about the debates, raised by Jamieson and Birdsell: "Do they test knowledge and vision? Do they sort good ideas from bad? Do they reveal important character traits and habits of mind to the voters? In short, do they provide voters with what they need to know to choose a president?"[5]

---

[1] PBS Newshour. "Debating our Destiny: Interview with Vice President Walter Mondale" (May 25, 1990), www.pbs.org/newshour/debatingourdestiny/interviews/mondale.html (accessed October 20, 2007).

[2] Kathleen Hall Jamieson and David S. Birdsell, *Presidential Debates: The Challenge of Creating an Informed Electorate* (New York: Oxford University Press, 1990), p. 5.

[3] Ibid., p. 4.

[4] Richard Nixon, *RN: The Memoirs of Richard Nixon* (New York: Grosset and Dunlap, 1978), p. 221.

[5] Jamieson and Birdsell, p. 6.

PRESIDENTIAL DEBATES: THEN AND NOW

1. A goal of this exercise is to help you learn what to look for while viewing this year's presidential debates. You will begin by viewing clips of past presidential debates. These clips show debate moments widely regarded as having an important impact on how voters saw the candidates, and on the final outcome of the election itself.

2. Begin by viewing a bit of perhaps the most famous presidential debate of all: the 1960 contest between John Kennedy and Richard Nixon. Go to **www.c-span.org/classroom/govt/debateshistory.asp.** You are at C-SPAN's website that provides transcripts of historical presidential debates. It also provides a short video clip of the 1960 debate.

3. Scroll down to the "Kennedy-Nixon" debate and click on **"watch clip."** As you watch, look for clues as to why most voters who saw this debate on TV thought that Kennedy had won (while it is reported that those who heard the debate on radio thought that Nixon had won). What do you see in the images that is more favorable to Kennedy?

Screenshot: www.cspan.org

Kennedy - Nixon Debate

On September 2... nedy of Massachusetts and Vice Preside... **Click here to watch** d in the first-ever televised presi... **the debate** precedent for all others to come... cans viewed this debate on television, many others ... ned in through the radio. Kennedy - Nixon History claims that more television viewer... believed Kennedy won, 1960 Debate while many radio listeners thought Nixon did. Watch Clip (4 min.) | Read Debate Transcript

4. *Based on this clip, which candidate appeared more appealing, at-ease, or otherwise attractive on the television? Explain your answer on the worksheet.* The 1960 debates were famous for offering a stark contrast of television *style and image*. This will be one of the items that will be included on your 2008 debate scorecard, at the end of this exercise.

5. Debates are also important for allowing voters to assess the knowledge level and substantive policy differences between candidates. To view a clip showing a serious policy discussion among candidates, go to **www.museum.tv/debateweb/html/greatdebate.**

6. You are now at the presidential debate archives of the Museum of Broadcast Communications. You can see that there are many resources on this webpage that you can explore if you are interested in the history of presidential debates. For this exercise, you are interested in the archive of video clips from past elections. Click on the link near the top of the webpage for **"Televised Debate History: 1960-2000."**

Screenshot: www.museum.tv

7. You are taken to a menu of presidential debates, broken down by year. To view the video clips for each year, you will click on the appropriate **"video"** link, which you can see in the screenshot below.

TELEVISED DEBATE HISTORY: 1960-2000

menu		
1960	video | photos | headlines | memos & spin	Select from the
1976	video | photos | headlines | memos & spin	in order to vi
1980	video | photos | headlines | memos & spin	headlines an
1984	video | photos | headlines | m	that year's pr

Screenshot: www.museum.tv

8. You will begin by viewing a video clip that shows a recent innovation in presidential debates: the "Town Hall" debate format. In "Town Hall" debates, candidates stand among and take questions from average voters (rather than from an appointed, formal moderator). In

this clip you will have a chance to reflect on how this format affects the feeling of the debate. You will also see how a debate can offer more sustained attention to policy issues than other election formats, such as the 30 second advertisement.

9. To view the clip, click on the **"video" link for the 1992 election.**

10. A list of available clips, with short descriptions, appears.

11. Scroll down to and click on the clip located under the **"Second Debate"** section, titled **"Town Hall Debate part 1,"** as seen in the screenshot. You will see a bit of a town hall debate between Republican George H. W. Bush, Democrat Bill Clinton, and Independent Ross Perot. They are debating free trade policy.

Screenshot: www.museum.tv

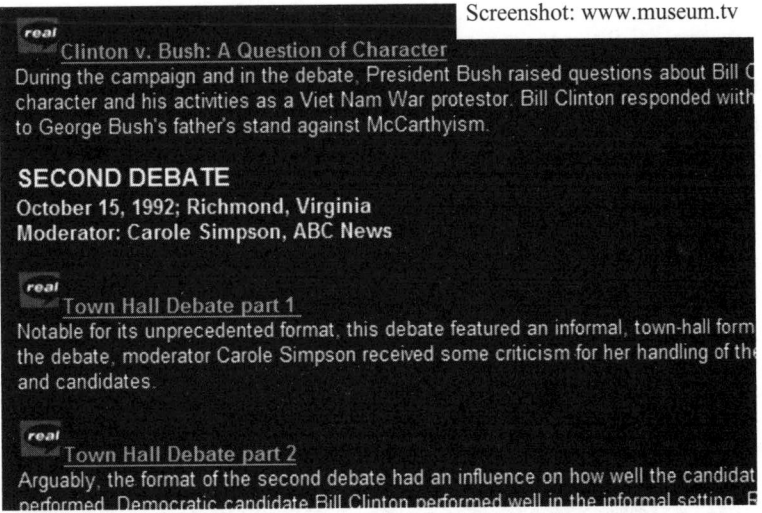

real Clinton v. Bush: A Question of Character
During the campaign and in the debate, President Bush raised questions about Bill C character and his activities as a Viet Nam War protestor. Bill Clinton responded wiith to George Bush's father's stand against McCarthyism.

SECOND DEBATE
October 15, 1992; Richmond, Virginia
Moderator: Carole Simpson, ABC News

real Town Hall Debate part 1
Notable for its unprecedented format, this debate featured an informal, town-hall form the debate, moderator Carole Simpson received some criticism for her handling of the and candidates.

real Town Hall Debate part 2
Arguably, the format of the second debate had an influence on how well the candidat performed. Democratic candidate Bill Clinton performed well in the informal setting. B

12. Now click on the second **"Town Hall Debate part 2"** clip from 1992. You will see a memorable debate moment. In this second clip, a voter directly challenges President Bush on an issue. The President seems flustered, while Bill Clinton has an entirely different style in his response. *How do you think the town hall format changes the dynamic of a presidential debate? Include your answer on the worksheet.*

13. Think about how the candidates' answers gave voters a detailed sense of policy stands on free trade. "Key Policy Issues" will be added to

your 2008 debate scorecard. "Format Effects" will also be added, so you can evaluate how the format of the 2008 debate helped or hurt the candidates. Throughout the rest of this exercise, the themes you explore will show up in the scorecard included after the worksheet.

14. "Attack and Response" is a key part of many debates. One candidate will attack the character, experience or ideas of the other candidate, and the attacked candidate must respond. An example is in **the 1992 debates.** Click on the link for **"Clinton v. Bush: A Question of Character."** This link is just above the links for the "Second Debate," and can be seen in the screenshot above, after step 11.

15. *Which candidate do you feel came out ahead in this example of "Attack and Response"? Why? Fill in your analysis on the worksheet.*

16. A sometimes devastating incident in debates is the grave or humorous mistake, otherwise known as the "gaffe." A gaffe can make a candidate appear foolish, or inadequate to the task of leading. In the 1976 debate, Gerald Ford made the gaffe of claiming that Eastern Europe was NOT under Soviet domination, although the facts showed otherwise. In the midst of the Cold War with the Soviets, it was a grave error that likely cost Ford votes and perhaps the presidency.

17. You can view the "No Soviet Domination" incident by going to the **1976 video clips** (as in step 9, above). When the list of clips appears, look for **"Ford's infamous gaffe"** clip in the second debate.

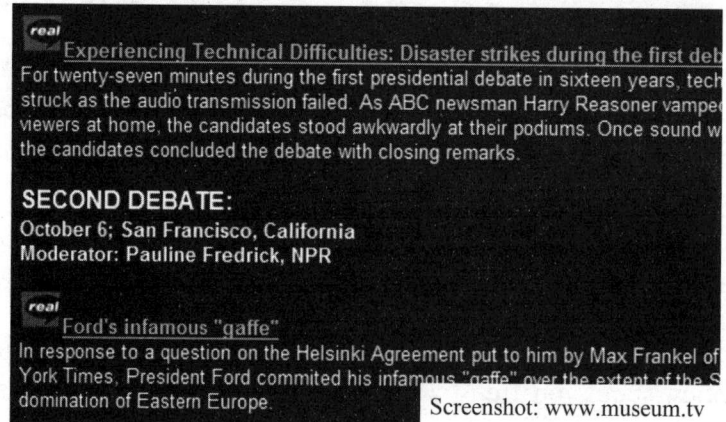

Screenshot: www.museum.tv

18. A more recent incident that might be considered a mistake or a gaffe by a candidate occurred in the 1988 election. In this case, Democratic candidate Dukakis (whom Republican candidate Bush was challenging as weak on crime) was asked whether he would want the death penalty if his own wife were raped and murdered. Dukakis's cold and rather dispassionate answer may have led voters to question whether he had the proper emotional "heart" to represent the people. View the clip by going to **the 1988 videos**, and scrolling down the clips under the "Second Debate." View the clip titled **"Dukakis v. Bernard Shaw."**

19. Sometimes debates achieve the opposite of the memorable mistake or gaffe; they result in a candidate delivering a celebrated and memorable "one-liner" or humorous bit. When a candidate delivers a perfect "soundbite" or bit of humor that captures the moment, voters and the press might talk about it for weeks (and remember it for years). Two examples of this phenomenon were delivered by Ronald Reagan. First in the 1980 election, Reagan delivered the famous question: "Are you better off than you were four years ago?" This question spoke to the anxieties of a nation with severe economic troubles and in the midst of the Iranian hostage crisis. Second, in the 1984 election, President Reagan (the oldest candidate ever to run for President) was being challenged as too old for the job. His humorous response put the issue to bed.

20. View the 1980 "Are you better off than you were four years ago?" one-liner by going to **the 1980 video clips.** Look for the "Second Debate" section and click on the clip for **"Reagan's closing remarks."** It is the final clip in the list.

21. View the 1984 clip of Reagan's humor by going to **the 1984 video clips** Go to the "Second Debate," and click on **"Reagan's response to the 'age question,'"** as seen in the screenshot below.

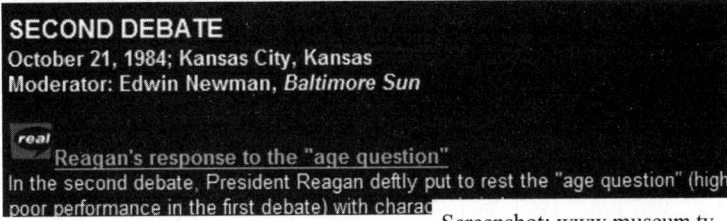

Screenshot: www.museum.tv

22. The final debate phenomenon that you will view could be called the "jujitsu" tactic. Jujitsu, a Japanese martial art, is the art of turning an opponent's energy and strength back against him or her. In a debate, jujitsu occurs when a candidate's particular strength, or a candidate's persuasive appeal to the voters, is powerfully turned back upon the candidate him- or herself, backfiring on the candidate in a surprising way. Done well, using jujitsu can devastate one's debate opponent and probably earn a candidate some support among the voters.

23. View a memorable episode of debate jujitsu by going to **the 1988 election clips.** Look for the "Vice-Presidential Debate." Then choose **"Bentsen on Quayle: No JFK."** This exchange has become legendary among political analysts for perfectly playing on Americans' lack of respect for the very young and arguably unaccomplished Dan Quayle as he ran for Vice President.

24. You can now judge which of these debate segments you just viewed is the most powerful, memorable or significant. *Choose ONE of the clips in the bullet list below and summarize on the worksheet why you think that clip was so memorable/significant in influencing the voters.*

   - Ford's Soviet domination gaffe
   - Dukakis and the death penalty
   - Reagan's "Are you better off" question
   - Reagan's joke about the age issue
   - Bentsen vs. Quayle: No JFK

25. Having viewed a variety of debate clips from 1960-1996, you have a better understanding of some key moments that played a role in past presidential elections. You also have a better understanding of the things you can look for in the 2008 presidential debate. Attached to this exercise is a "Presidential Debate Scorecard" based on some of the themes of this exercise. If your instructor advises you to use it, you can use this scorecard to take notes during the presidential debates, and/or to help in discussing the debate with your classmates after it is over.

Done!

PRESIDENTIAL DEBATES WORKSHEET

1. Which candidate was more appealing in the 1960 debate? Why?

2. How does the town hall format influence the dynamic of a debate?

3. Which candidate benefited from the Clinton/Bush attack? Why?

4. What video clip did you find most memorable? Why?

Presidential Debate Scorecard

	Republican	Democrat
Style and Image		
Format Effects (Who benefited most from the format?)		
Key Policy Issue or Display of Knowledge		
Attack/Response or Gaffe/Mistake		
Key One-Liner or Humorous Moment		
Campaign Jujitsu		
Overall: Who Benefited Most from the Debate? Why?		

Folk wisdom has it that politicians can hardly be trusted more than used car salesmen. A variety of polls show a decline in recent decades in such things as trust in elected officials and the percent of people believing that elections make a difference. Only about 50% (and often less) of the population bothers to vote in federal elections. Asked why, many Americans claim they are turned off by politics and politicians. It hasn't always been this way. Approval ratings of politicians were once much higher (in the 1950s and 1960s, for example), as were voting rates.

What is to blame for this dismal state of affairs? Have politicians truly become more degraded, causing people to tune out? Are voters today more spoiled and apathetic?

In a classic study published fifteen years ago, scholar Thomas Patterson blames neither the politicians nor the voters: he blames the media. Media coverage of elections is increasingly "Out of Order," Patterson argues.[1] The problem is that media coverage, which shapes how voters see politicians and elections, is increasingly negative and cynical, according to Patterson. Voters want to look at elections as opportunities to address problems, initiate policies, and elect quality leaders. But the media tends to report elections as strategic games, played by manipulative candidates, whose every move is geared not toward addressing problems but toward winning the support of voters.

Patterson argues that while voters look toward candidates' policy positions and wonder how those policies might affect their lives and the health of their country, the media analyzes these policy positions from a "games" perspective—who is the candidate trying to persuade, or fool, with this new policy stance? While voters hope to discover a quality leader, with skills and values that the voter can respect, most press coverage is negative, tearing down candidates and highlighting scandals.

Patterson argues that as voters experience this kind of coverage, they turn off from politics and politicians. With each election cycle, according to Patterson, the media's tendency toward horse-race/scandal coverage grows and the amount of attention given to serious policy/leadership style coverage shrinks. No wonder our election system is increasingly "Out of Order."

In this exercise, you will have a chance to update Patterson's findings— now about fifteen years old. Has the media tendency toward horse-race/negative-scandal coverage grown worse since 1993? Does the media tend to cover elections by educating voters about the policy issues being debated and the leadership skills of the various candidates, or does election coverage focus mostly on the election games being played by the candidates, on negative attacks, and on scandals? As a case study to help you answer this question, you will analyze the coverage in America's leading daily newspaper, the *New York Times*.

---

[1] Thomas Patterson. *Out of Order* (Vintage: New York, 1993).

EVALUATING THE MEDIA

1. Patterson argues that voters want more serious policy and leadership coverage from the media, but mostly what they get it is horse-race and negative/scandal coverage. Before you examine the media coverage to see if he is correct, it is important that you have a sense of what counts as *"horse-race/games"* coverage, what counts as *"negative/scandal"* coverage, what counts as *"policy"* coverage, and what counts as *"quality of leadership"* coverage. There is no precise way to judge a news article as one or the other of these types of coverage, so scholars use what is called "content analysis." Essentially, this means that the scholar (*you*, in this exercise) simply reads the article and makes a fair judgment about the overall thrust of the article, based on its topic (focused on policy or polls?), its tone (positive or negative toward the candidate?), and its overall point (is the article analyzing how a policy would affect voters, or is it analyzing how a proposed policy helps or hurts the candidate in the game to attract votes?).

2. Many times, articles will include *both* policy coverage and games coverage, or they might focus on both leadership style *and* the game of winning an election. But often, articles will have an overall thrust that fits best into one of the four categories described here. Your job will be to assess where each article fits, based on your best judgment.

3. A simple guide on how to categorize articles is presented on the following pages. Read over the sample article segments and you should see how they lead the article to being categorized as either a "Horse-race/Games" article, a "Negative/Scandal" article or a "Policy/Leadership" article. In later stages of this exercise, you will read and categorize *New York Times* articles on your own.

Horse-race/Games Coverage

This kind of article focuses on the race to attract voters. It may focus on who is ahead or behind in the polls. It might interpret recent policy ideas, or a candidate's speech, in terms of how this policy or speech was designed to attract certain groups of voters. These articles are about how candidates are playing the election game, and who is winning or losing.

Excerpted Examples of "Horse-race/Games" Coverage

Republicans Trail Democrats in Fund-Raising
New York Times, July 4, 2007 (A. Nagourney)

The top three Democrats, including former Senator John Edwards of North Carolina, raised $68.5 million over the past three months, compared with $48.7 million for the top three Republicans... Since the start of the year, the Democrats raised nearly 50 percent more than the Republicans, $144.3 million compared with $101.7 million.

With Husband, Clinton tries to revive Iowa Bid
New York Times, July 3, 2007 (P. Healy and A. Nagourney)

Former President Bill Clinton was at his wife's side on Monday for the first time in her campaign in Iowa, assuming a new political role: that of a helpmate seeking to raise Senator Hillary Rodham Clinton's standing in a politically important state where her bid for the presidency appears to be struggling. In a new and delicate strategy for Mrs. Clinton's candidacy, the former president, arguably the most popular leader in the Democratic Party has been dispatched to position her for the Iowa caucuses in January without upstaging her as she seeks to stake her own claim on leadership. Mrs. Clinton has been trailing in the Iowa polls behind former Senator John Edwards, and at times she has run third after Senator Barack Obama as well. The effort to overcome the slow start got under way in earnest on Monday night when, standing on bales of hay and surrounded by several thousand people at the Iowa State Fairgrounds here, she and her husband held hands as they waved, their smiles wide.

Negative/Scandal coverage

This kind of article focuses on scandals or similar negative episodes. The article might highlight negative historical facts about a candidate (such as rumors of affairs or improper handling of money), or might focus on a misstep or "gaffe" made by the candidate (an unwise racial remark, a blunder in speech phrasing, a misstep by top campaign advisors).

Excerpted Example of "Negative/Scandal" Coverage

Edwards's Hair Stylist Takes It From the Top
Washington Post, July 4, 2007 (J. Solomon)

At first, [John Edwards'] haircuts were free. But because Torrenueva often had to fly somewhere on the campaign trail to meet his client, he began charging $300 to $500 for each cut, plus the cost of airfare and hotels when he had to travel outside California. Torrenueva said one haircut during the 2004 presidential race cost $1,250 because he traveled to Atlanta and lost two days of work....Edwards, however, has been unusually susceptible to mockery. Before the $400 haircut, his campaign had to deal with the YouTube video in which he was captured primping for the camera...

Policy Coverage

This kind of article focuses on policy stances of a candidate. It analyzes the policies a candidate stands for, and might include analysis of how these policies could affect voters.

Excerpted Example of "Policy" Coverage

Domestic Issues Frame Democratic Debate
New York Times, June 29, 2007 (A. Nagourney and J. Zeleney)

For 90 minutes Thursday night, eight Democratic candidates debated before an audience made up largely of one of their party's most reliable and liberal constituencies, African-American voters, and used the stage to urge a revitalization of domestic programs they said had faltered under President Bush.

They called for spending more on schools in poor neighborhoods to lower class sizes and raising salaries for teachers to prevent a drain of educators from inner-city schools. They called for rolling back tax cuts on the wealthy to pay for expanded health care and provide job training...The foreign policy issue of the night was how to end the genocide in Darfur; the candidates generally agreed that the policies of the Bush administration have neglected the crisis there...Issues of crime and punishment also were raised, with each of the candidates calling for an end to racial disparities in sentencing laws and policing.

Leadership Coverage

This kind of article primarily focuses on the kind of leader a candidate might be. It may examine the leadership style of candidates, might look into their ability to build coalitions, or might explore the core values of a candidate.

Excerpted Example of "Leadership" Coverage

Romney Questioned by Conservatives
The Washington Post, June 30, 2007 (M. Glover, AP)

GOP presidential hopeful Mitt Romney, courting Iowa conservatives, found himself answering questions Saturday about the role his Mormon faith would play should he win the race. Romney told one questioner at a forum co-sponsored by a Christian group that "we have exactly the same values" and said there is no religious litmus test for candidates. The former Massachusetts governor dismissed suggestions of a conflict between his religion and his ability to govern. He also hastened to offer assurances of his faith.

"The Bible for me is the word of God," Romney said. "I also believe that Jesus Christ is my savior. ... It is essential that we have a Republican president who is pro-life and pro-family," said Romney.

4. Now that you have a sense of how to categorize articles, you are ready to evaluate the election coverage. Go to **www.nytimes.com.**

5. Your screen will look something like this. If you haven't done so already, click on the link (top right) to **"Register Now."** You do not have to pay to register for basic access to the online New York Times.

Screenshot: www.nytimes.com. © New York Times Co., Inc. Used with permission.

6. After you have registered, if you are not automatically logged in, click the link to **"Log In"** (top right of page). Now, click the link to **"Politics"** on the far left of the page.

Screenshot: www.nytimes.com. © New York Times Co., Inc. Used with permission.

7. You will be taken to the "Politics" section, where you can review articles on the presidential election. While reviewing the articles, you can assign each one a score as either a "policy/leadership style" article (which Patterson says voters want to read) or a "horse-race/ scandal" article (which Patterson says the media gives us too much of).

8. The "Politics" section of the *New York Times* looks like the screenshots below. You should evaluate the regular news coverage, and NOT the informal and gossipy "blogs" that are also on this page. Therefore, **AVOID** the first part of this page (called "The Caucus: Latest posts from our politics blog"), and examine the articles found in the section below the blogs (the **"Latest News"** section). The articles in the actual news section will have bylines (author's names) attached to them, so look for those in choosing articles for your analysis.

Screenshot: www.nytimes.com

Screenshot: www.nytimes.com. © New York Times Co., Inc.
Used with permission.

9. There will be a list of links to articles available for your review in this **"Latest News"** section. You should be able to tell from the titles which articles are focused on the 2008 presidential election.

10. Click the link for the first relevant article you see. When the article appears, read it over and assign it to one of three categories:

    - **Horserace/Games or Negative/Scandal.** If the article is mostly about the game of winning the election, OR about a negative/scandalous development, place it in this category.

    - **Policy/Leadership.** If the article is mostly about the policies proposed by candidates OR about the leadership style and values of the candidates, place it in this category.

    - **Balanced/Other.** If the article is balanced between horserace/scandal and policy/leadership issues, or if it is about some entirely different issue that can't be categorized for this exercise, assign it to this category.

11. Repeat this process for **at least** twelve articles. If you run out of news articles, you can use some of the blog posts discussed in step 8, above.

12. *Figure out the percentage of articles you placed in each category, and fill in the worksheet.* You can determine percentages by dividing the number of articles in a category by the total number of articles you reviewed (example: if you placed 4 articles in the policy category, you would divide 4 by 12—the overall number of articles—and come up with .3, or 30%). Based on a very limited sample (**not** a representative sample!), you now know the percentage of *New York Times* articles that focus on Horserace/Scandal, the percentage that focus on Policy/ Leadership issues, and the percentage that do not easily fit into either category. *On your worksheet, you can now evaluate if Patterson's*

1992 findings continue to be accurate for this small sample. Also include your reflections on the quality of New York Times *coverage of the presidential race.*

13. *Attach the following materials to your worksheet before turning it in:*

- Print a good example of one article that you placed in each category.

- Label the articles with the category you placed them into.

- Highlight one or two paragraphs that most led you to your conclusion.

Done!

EVALUATING THE MEDIA WORKSHEET

	Horserace or Negative/ Scandal	Policy/ Leadership	Balanced/ Other
Percent of Articles in the *New York Times*			

1. Does your data confirm or contradict Patterson's hypothesis? What are your thoughts on whether there is too much negative/games coverage in elections reporting?

2. Based on this review, would you say the *New York Times* does a good job educating voters about the presidential election? Why or why not? Your answer does not have to agree with Patterson that Horserace/Games or Negative/Scandal coverage is bad; for example, you could argue that voters need to know such things in order to make good choices.

3. Attach one example of each kind of article, as explained in step 13 of this exercise.

Back in 1884, everyone was talking about the Mugwumps: Republican activists who voted for Democratic presidential candidate Grover Cleveland (due to outrage at scandal within the Republican Party), and who won the election for the Democrats by swinging the critical state of New York. This critical voter group switched between the Republicans and the Democrats so were portrayed in newspapers as fence-sitters with their face ("mug") on one side and their rear-end ("wump") on the other: Mugwumps. What critical voter group or groups will play a vital role in the 2008 election, and what will they be called?

Vital voter groups emerge in every election, and often one or more of these groups are remembered as having played the decisive role in determining winners and losers. Many argue that the 2004 election was determined by a surge of church-going, socially conservative voters toward Bush. These voters were motivated by concerns over such things as abortion, gay marriage, and cultural indecency and they wanted a president who prioritized his relationship with God: they were called the "Values Voters." Another much talked about group in 2004 was the "Security Moms." Some evidence suggested that women voters with children were especially concerned with protecting their families from terrorist attacks, and thus voted for Bush as the more trusted of the two candidates on protecting the nation from future attacks.

Back in the 1990s, "Security Moms" were nowhere to be seen. Instead, we had the "Soccer Moms." Pollsters argued that middle to upper-class, suburban, married women with children (who had to shuttle children to soccer practice) were concerned with such things as affordable health care, rising college tuition, and uncertain job prospects that were undermining the economic security of their families. Therefore, the "Soccer Moms" in 1996 tilted to Democrat Bill Clinton and helped him win the presidency.

What about the "NASCAR Dads"? These are blue-collar, sports-loving, patriotic men (often from the South and usually white) who were credited with helping propel George W. Bush to victory. In the 1980s, we had the "Reagan Democrats": former Democratic voters, often from union families or heavily Democratic states, who began voting Republican during the Reagan years due to their disdain for an increasingly liberal Democratic Party and concern over their worsening economic situation.

Election candidates and their consultants constantly discuss what voter groups are most critical in any given election, and seek to understand what concerns are moving these voters. For example, if Democratic consultants feel that angry "Reagan Democrats" are abandoning their party, they will likely urge their candidates to shift to the right and talk more like Republicans in order to win the Reagan Democrats back. Similarly, for students of elections, a study of such voter groups lends insight into the nature of the American electorate. Which voter groups are emerging to move the nation left or right? What concerns are Americans expressing?

When the 2008 election is over, which voter groups will we remember as having defined this election season? Will we be talking about how young "Generation Next" voters emerged as a cohesive voter bloc, with high turnout and a strong anti-war sentiment? Will scholars discover that affluent, bohemian urban professionals (perhaps called "Buppies") played a key role in voting for candidates matching their values of economic self-confidence and social tolerance? Maybe a surge in Latino voting will lead campaign consultants to ponder Latinos and their policy preferences. What about the "You-Tubers" and the High-tech "Wired Workers"? They might emerge as definitive voter groups with concerns all their own.

In this exercise, you will analyze 2004 and 2006 exit-polling data to determine which voter groups were definitive in those elections. You will also analyze a variety of 2008 data sources to predict a key voter group that is emerging in 2008, and give that group a catchy name.

KEY VOTER GROUPS

1. Begin your work by exploring voter dynamics from 2004. CNN maintains a good archive of 2004 exit poll data. Go to **www.cnn.com/ELECTION/2004/pages/results/states/US/P/00/**. You will see a link to find the full exit poll data to the right of this page. Click on "**voter survey results**" as in the screenshot below.

| | TING HEDULE | | STILL VOTING | | PROCESSING RESULTS | | TOO CLOSE TO CALL | | PARTY CONTROL CHANGED | | COUNTY MAP | PARTY KEY |

Full President ›

	CANDIDATE	VOTE	VOTE %	PRECINCTS	LOCAL	EXIT POLLS
R	**Bush** (Incumbent)	62,040,606	**51%**	**100%** of precincts reporting	not available	voter survey results
D	**Kerry**	59,028,109	**48%**			
I	**Nader**	411,304	**1%**			

Screenshot: www.cnn.com

2. The exit poll data appears. As you scroll through the data, you can see how different categories of voters broke down in terms of whether they were heavily Bush (Republican) or Kerry (Democrat), or whether they were balanced. There are also tips on how to read the data.

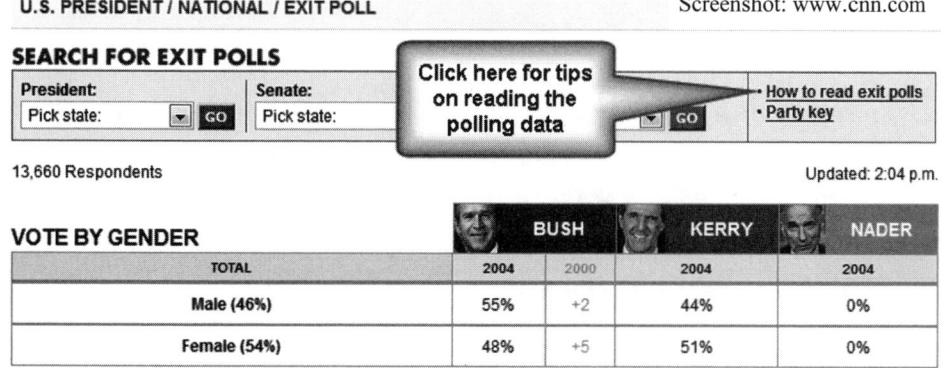

U.S. PRESIDENT / NATIONAL / EXIT POLL   Screenshot: www.cnn.com

SEARCH FOR EXIT POLLS

| President: | Senate: | Click here for tips on reading the polling data | | • How to read exit polls • Party key |

Pick state: GO   Pick state: GO

13,660 Respondents   Updated: 2:04 p.m.

VOTE BY GENDER	BUSH		KERRY	NADER
TOTAL	2004	2000	2004	2004
Male (46%)	55%	+2	44%	0%
Female (54%)	48%	+5	51%	0%

3. The first column of data (i.e., the column that has headers like "vote by gender," or "vote by race and gender,") contains categories of voters (such as "White Men" or "White Women"). Each category is followed by a percentage, such as "White Men (36%)." The percentage figure is the number of all voters polled who were within that specific category—for example, 36% of all voters polled were white men. That gives you a sense of how large each voter category is.

4. Spend some time exploring the categories of voters that this data provides and analyzing how different groups voted.

5. Based on this exploration, determine one group of voters that was a large percent of the electorate, and that was a key voting bloc for Bush, showing significantly more support for the Republican candidate than for Kerry. For example, if you scroll down the webpage you can see that 43% of all voters polled felt the economy was in "good" shape, and that 87% of such voters voted for Bush.

NATIONAL ECONOMY		BUSH		KERRY
TOTAL	2004	2000	2004
Excellent (4%)	89%	+63	11%
Good (43%)	87%	+35	13%
Not Good (35%)	26%	-36	72%
Poor (17%)	6%		

Screenshot: www.cnn.com

6. *Find your own example of a similar large group that was heavily pro-Bush and list that group on the attached worksheet. Add a sentence or two about why you think this group might have voted so heavily for the Republican candidate.* You have just performed a bit of political scholarship, dissecting and explaining election results.

7. Repeat step 5 for Kerry, the Democratic candidate. Except this time, find a group that is a relatively *small* portion of the electorate (under 25%) and that voted heavily for the Democrat. *List that group on the*

worksheet, and include a bit of analysis about why you think this unique group voted as it did. You have just discovered a segment of the electorate that future Democrats might want to target for voter outreach and turnout efforts—but strategists have to be careful in dedicating resources to such groups, since they are so small.

8. Now that you have a better understanding of key voter groups in the 2004 presidential election, you can apply the same kind of analysis to the 2006 congressional elections in which the Democrats took control of Congress from the Republicans.

9. Go to **www.cnn.com/ELECTION/2006/pages/results/states/US/**. Please note that this link is different than the link in step 1, in that you are going to the **2006 results,** not the 2004 results. Once there, click the **"voter survey results"** link as you did in step 1.

10. Like the 2004 data, this data breaks voters down into various categories and then shows how each category broke down in terms of whether the voters in that group voted for a Democratic or a Republican candidate for the House of Representatives. This data covers how voters in *all* House races across the nation voted. In the screenshot below, you can see that 51% of all voters were female, and that 55% of these female voters voted for Democrats.

U.S. HOUSE OF REPRESENTATIVES / NATIONAL / EXIT POLL

13,251 Respondents

Screenshot: www.cnn.com

VOTE BY GENDER

TOTAL	Democrat	Republican
Male (49%)	50%	47%
Female (51%)	55%	43%

11. Repeat the analysis that you did for the 2004 election. Find a part of the electorate that was heavily Republican, and a different segment of the voters that was heavily Democrat. *On the worksheet, list those groups, their percent of the electorate, and their voting pattern.*

12. Think about why each group might have voted as it did, and what kind of national mood or movement the group may represent. Based on your reflection, come up with a clever name to attach to each group—a name that the news dailies and TV talking heads can use in their attention grabbing headlines. As noted earlier, past names of important voting groups include such clever taglines as "Mugwumps," "Values Voters," "Soccer Moms" and "NASCAR Dads." What name can you devise to sum up your group and grab the reader's attention? For example, toward the bottom of this website you can see that 12% of the voters are not confident that votes are counted fairly, and that 72% of those voters chose Democrats. You might call this group the "Conspiracy Theorists," or (if you were a tongue-in-cheek staffer working for the Republican Party), the "Lunatic Left."

Come up with your own names and list them in the worksheet. Now you are not only a political scholar, but are on your way to marketing the next great tagline for understanding the American electorate.

13. Now you are ready to apply this same kind of analysis to dissecting polling data from the current 2008 presidential election. Your task will be to visit a variety of polling/public opinion websites and, based on what you learn there, to identify and name a key group that is shaping up as vital in this election and to analyze what kind of issue or issues are moving them. This time you will not be looking backward to explain past elections, but looking forward to predict the upcoming election.

14. Begin by familiarizing yourself with the data at the widely respected "Cook Report." Go to **www.cookpolitical.com.**

15. Select the **"Presidential Race"** button to the left of the screen to find polling data and analysis of what it means. Below the "Presidential Race" button, you can click the **"Cook Political Report"** button for more data. Spend some time exploring the resources here, and learning from Cook's perspective.

16. Now that you have a more sophisticated sense of the lay of the land, feel free to explore the wide variety of other political polling websites with good public opinion data. Remember your task is not just to discover the percent of all people supporting one or the other presidential candidate. Rather you are looking to discover a *unique group of the electorate* (e.g., church-going evangelicals or young Latinos) that seems to breaking heavily toward one or the other candidate, and/or that is clearly voicing a unique concern about public policy that is likely to affect their final vote (e.g., you might find that young Latinos are 4% of the electorate and that 80% of them will be voting based on the immigration issue—you could call this voting group the "Latino Surge" or some such thing).

17. Here are some good public opinion/polling data websites. There are many other good sites available, and this list is simply suggestive. Visit a few sites (you may depart from this list if you wish), and you will find the kind of data you need.

   - *New York Times* Pollwatch:
     www.nytimes.com/ref/us/polls_index.html

   - Washington Post polls: www.washingtonpost.com/wp-dyn/content/politics/polls/index.html

   - CBS news polls:
     www.cbsnews.com/sections/opinion/polls/main500160.shtml

   - A vast collection of polls: www.pollingreport.com

   - Longtime polling leader—explore the articles and polls in the "Politics" section: www.gallup.com/

   - Rasmussen Report polls:
     www.rasmussenreports.com/public_content/politics

18. Based on this research, identify a specific group in the electorate (if possible, also identify how large that group is, as a percent of all voters), identify the issue that seems to be moving them (relying either on hard polling data or thoughtful personal conjecture), and come up with a clever name for your group. If you can find the right data, also identify which candidate your group seems to be moving toward. *Present all of this data in questions six and seven in the worksheet.*

Done!

KEY VOTER GROUPS WORKSHEET

	2004 Voter Group that you chose to analyze	What percent of all voters does this group represent?	What percent of these voters voted for Bush or for Kerry?
Pro-Bush voters			
Pro-Kerry voters			

1. Why do you think the pro-Bush voters voted as they did?

2. Why do you think the pro-Kerry voters as they did?

3. List a group of voters that was heavily Republican in 2006, and provide the percentage of this group that voted Republican.

4. List a segment of the electorate that was heavily Democratic in 2006, and provide the percentage of this group that voted Democrat.

5. Give a clever name to each group you identified in questions 3-4.

Republican	
Democrat	

6. Identify an important voter group in 2008, describe the issue that seems to be moving them, and give the group a clever name.

7. Which candidate does your group seem to be moving toward? Why do you think that is?

ISSUE ELEVEN
WAS THERE A MANDATE?

"No concept invokes the connection between the public and the president more than the electoral mandate, for it implies that the president shall work to make the will of the people into law."[1] Frequently, presidential election victors claim a "mandate" from the people to implement specific policies and to lead Congress in general. For example, on election night 1980, the vice-president- elect claimed that Ronald Reagan's victory was

> "not simply a mandate for change, but a mandate for peace and freedom; a mandate for prosperity; a mandate for opportunity for all Americans...a mandate to make government the servant of the people in the way our founding fathers intended;...a mandate for hope of fulfillment of the great dream that President-elect Reagan has worked for all his life."[2]

President Bush celebrated his 2004 victory with similar claims:

> ...when you win, there is a feeling that the people have spoken and embraced your point of view... the people made it clear what they wanted... I've earned capital in this camp and now I intend to use it...I'm going to spend it for what I told the people I'd spend it on, which is — you've heard the agenda: Social Security and tax reform, moving this economy forward, education, fighting and winning the war on terror.[3]

Many scholars are skeptical of the idea of a "presidential mandate." How can there be a mandate, when voters are usually ignorant about the policy goals of candidates, campaigns are driven by simplistic 30 second ads, and the results of the election are usually "noisy and ambiguous as signals of the electorate's concerns and intentions"?[4]

Still others point out that it doesn't really matter whether or not voters truly meant to support a specific "mandate" for change. Even if voters aren't informed and united enough to support a specific agenda, leaders in Congress and across the land often *believe* that voters support the president-elect's policies. If other politicians act on their perceptions of a mandate by supporting the president's policies, then it is same as if the mandate were a real fact.[5]

Claims of a presidential mandate, therefore, are important. If a mandate truly exists, it allows voters to express their desires through presidential leadership. And whether or not voters are united behind a presidential mandate, Presidents often claim they are. When politicians and pundits rally around these claims, it helps the President to advance his policies.

But not all elections are interpreted by politicians and pundits as delivering a mandate. Some elections, like FDR's 1932 victory and Reagan's 1980 victory, are widely seen as delivering a clear message from the voters—while many others are seen only as politics as usual. Will the election of 2008 be remembered as delivering a historic mandate to the presidential victor, or as just another normal presidential election? You will explore that question in this exercise by examining: the scope of the President's election victory, congressional election results, key voter groups and policy issues in the election, and the "conventional wisdom" among the pundits and the press—do they *think* a mandate was delivered?

---

[1] Patricia Heidotting Conley. *Presidential Mandates: How Elections Shape the National Agenda* (Chicago: University of Chicago Press, 2001) p. 1.

[2] Quoted in Robert Dahl. "Myth of the Presidential Mandate" *Political Science Quarterly* 105 (1990): p. 355.

[3] President Bush. "President Holds Press Conference," www.whitehouse.gov/news/releases/2004/11/20041104-5.html (accessed November 4, 2007).

[4] Conley, p. 23.

[5] Lawrence J. Grossback, et. al. "Comparing Competing Theories on the Causes of Mandate Perceptions" *American Journal of Political Science* 49 (2005): pp. 406-419.

WAS THERE A MANDATE?

1. Many scholars point out that mandates emerge when several conditions occur. These conditions include:

    - The president's scope of victory is strong (i.e., the president wins by a large margin).

    - The president's party registers strong gains in Congress.

    - New voter groups emerge in dramatic fashion (or shifting loyalties transform existing voting groups).

    - Policy signals from voters are strong and clear.

    - Among the press and officials, a consensus or "conventional wisdom" emerges that the President has won a mandate.

    In this exercise, you will explore whether these conditions were present in the 2008 election.

2. Begin by examining the President's scope of victory. For an election to be considered a mandate, the size of the President's victory must be large, compared to other elections. You can examine the size of victories in previous elections by going to **www.presidency.ucsb.edu**.

3. You are now at "The American Presidency Project" of John Woolley and Gerhard Peters of the University of California at Santa Barbara. If you click on the "**elections**" button in the menu at the top of the page, you see a list of election years that you can explore, calling up maps and other data for various election years, if you wish.

4. You can also see a comprehensive list of data from *all* presidential elections by clicking on the "**data**" button, as in the screenshot on the next page. Do that now.

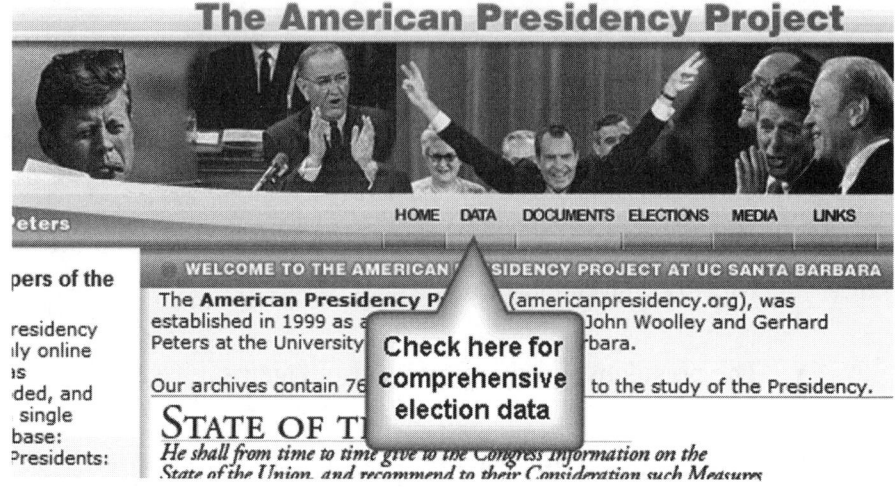

Screenshot: Gerhard Peters and John T. Woolley, *The American Presidency*   3
Project, UC Santa Barbara, www.presidency.ucsb.edu. Used with permisssion.

5. You are taken to a list of data archives related to the presidency. For this exercise, you are interested in the archive on **"Popular and Electoral Vote Mandates,"** which is in the **"Presidential Selection"** section of the page. Scroll down the page to select this link.

Growth of the Executive Branch
 ◆ Federal Budget Receipts and Outlays
 ◆ Differences in Appropriations Proposed by P...
 ◆ Executive Orders
 ◆ White House Staff Budget
 ◆ Size of the Executive Office of the President

Click here for data on the size of various election victories

Presidential Selection
 ◆ Popular and Electoral Vote Mandates
 ◆ Representation of President's Party in House Elections
 ◆ Voter Turnout in Presidential Elections
 ◆ Election Year Presidential Preferences Over Time
 ◆ Financing Presidential General Elections
 ◆ % of Convention Delegates Selected through Primary Elections Democratic | R...

Screenshot: Gerhard Peters and John T. Woolley, *The American Presidency*
Project, UC Santa Barbara, www.presidency.ucsb.edu. Used with permission.

6. After clicking on the link, you are taken to charts showing the size of election victories through history. Study these charts to get a sense of several "landslide" victories that are widely regarded as delivering popular mandates, versus other elections that are not interpreted this way. Particularly examine the data in the following elections, which have all been argued to have delivered popular mandates:

- Franklin Roosevelt's 1932 and 1936 elections
- Lyndon Johnson's 1964 election
- Richard Nixon's 1972 election
- Ronald Reagan's 1980 and 1984 elections

7. Below the raw data on this webpage, there are graphs of the data. As you can see in the graph of **"electoral vote advantage"** (which compares the percentage of all electoral votes captured by the winning candidate to those captured by the loser), there is a real difference between landslide or "mandate" elections (circled by this workbook's author in the screenshot below) and other elections.

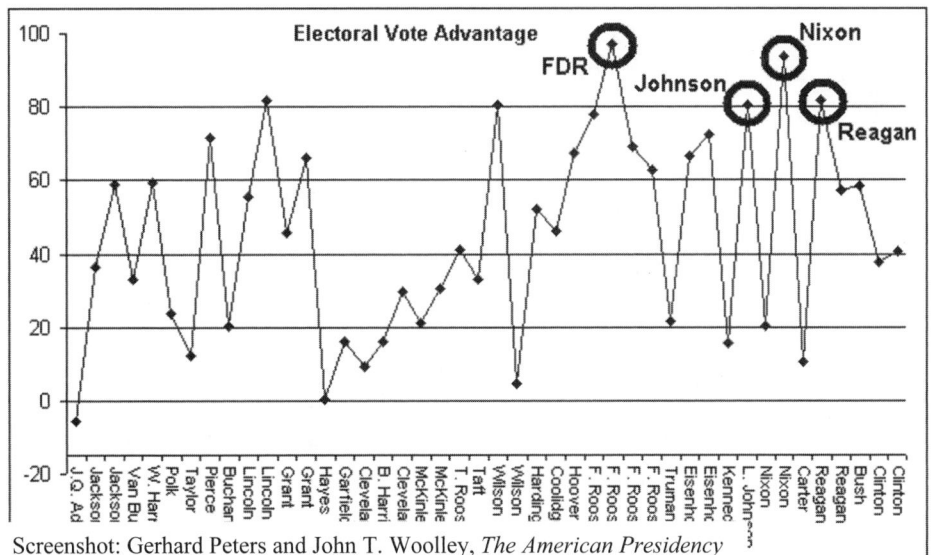

Screenshot: Gerhard Peters and John T. Woolley, *The American Presidency Project*, UC Santa Barbara, www.presidency.ucsb.edu. Used with permission.

8. To help you determine whether the 2008 presidential victory was a historically unusual "mandate" election similar to these other landslide elections, you need to determine the average size of "normal" popular vote and electoral college victories, and the average size of "mandate election" victories—so that you can compare the two. For the purposes of this exercise, the calculations on the historical data have already been done for you. Here are the results.

	Normal Election	Mandate Election
Popular Vote Advantage*	5.4%	16.6%
Percent of Electoral Votes*	66%	94%

Popular Vote Advantage = Percent of all popular votes won by the winning candidate MINUS the percent of popular votes won by the loser.

Percent of Electoral Votes = Percent of all Electoral College votes won by the winning candidate.

9. Now that you know how "normal" election margins compare to "mandate" elections, you can compare the data to the 2008 results.

10. Using data on the popular vote breakdown that you can find with a basic Internet search, determine the "Popular Vote Advantage" of the winning presidential candidate in 2008. You can do this by simply subtracting the percent of the popular vote won by the losing candidate from the percent of the popular vote won by the winning candidate. For example, if "Winning Candidate A" received 54% of the vote, and "Losing Candidate B" received 46% of the vote, you would subtract 46 from 54 to come up with a 9% Popular Vote Advantage. *Fill this information into your worksheet.*

11. Now determine the percent of all Electoral College votes won by the winning presidential candidate in 2008. You do this by simply dividing all the Electoral College votes won by the winning candidate by the total number of electoral colleges existing (538). For example, if the winning candidate won 300 electoral votes, you would divide

300 by 538 and come up with .557, or 55.7%. *Determine your answer and fill in the information on the worksheet.*

12. On the worksheet, you can see how the numbers from the 2008 election compare to the historical data from "normal" elections and to the data from unusual "landslide" or "mandate" elections. Based just on this comparison, does the 2008 election meet the standards for a mandate election or not? *Fill in the answer on your worksheet.*

13. The scale of the presidential victory in the popular vote and Electoral College is just one way to measure a presidential mandate. Another measure is the scale of the gains made by the President's party in Congress. If the President's party gained many seats in Congress, the election is more likely to be called a mandate.

14. To determine if the number of congressional seats gained or lost by the President's party in the 2008 election is historically unusual, you need to determine the average number of seats gained in Congress by the President's party in "mandate" elections versus the average number of seats gained for the President's party in "normal" elections. Because only one-third of Senate seats turn over each election, you will only examine turnover in the House of Representatives.

15. The historical numbers you need have already been calculated for you in this exercise, according to the following assumptions. "Mandate" elections in modern times are assumed to be Franklin Roosevelt in 1932 and 1936, Lyndon Johnson in 1964, Richard Nixon in 1972, and Ronald Reagan in 1980 and 1984. **The average number of House seats gained by the President-elect's party in these "mandate" elections was 39. In all other presidential elections since 1932, the average number of House seats gained by the President-elect's party was 8.**

16. Though you don't have to complete this step for this exercise, you may view the data utilized to determine the figures in step 14 by going to **http://en.wikipedia.org/wiki/Elections_in_the_United_States**. A great

database of historic election data is maintained here. Scroll down towards the bottom of the page and you will see links to data from every congressional election (see screenshot).

United States presidential elections

) | 1824 | 1828 | 1832 | 1836 | 1840 | 1844 | 1848 | 1852 | 1856 | 1860 | 1864 | 1868 | 1872 | 1876 | 1880 | 1884 |
3 | 1940 | 1944 | 1948 | 1952 | 1956 | 1960 | 1964 | 1968 | 1972 | 1976 | 1980 | 1984 | 1988 | 1992 | 1996 | 2000 |

See also: House | Senate | Governors

United States House of Representatives Elections

I | 1806 | 1808 | 1810 | 1812 | 1814 | 1816 | 1818 | 1820 | 1822 | 1824 | 1826 | 1828 | 1830 | 1832 | 1834 | 1836 |
) | 1872 | 1874 | 1876 | 1878 | 1880 | 1882 | 1884 | 1886 | 1888 | 1890 | 1892 | 1894 | 1896 | 1898 | 1900 | 1902 |
3 | 1938 | 1940 | 1942 | 1944 | 1946 | 1948 | 1950 | 1952 | 1954 | 1956 | 1958 | 1960 | 1962 | 1964 | 1966 | 1968 |
1986 | 1988 | 1990 | 1992 | 1994 | 1996 | 1998 | 2000 | 2002 | 2004 | 2006 | 2008 | Special

See also: Senate | President | Gover Screenshot: http://en.wikipedia.org

17. Now that you know the average number of House seats gained by the president-elect's party in a "mandate" election (39) and the average seats gained in a "normal" election (8), you can determine whether the number of House seats gained (or lost) by the president-elect in the 2008 election can be considered evidence of a mandate or not.

18. Using any source, determine how many seats the President-elect's party gained or lost in the House of Representatives in 2008. *Report this number on your worksheet, and add your assessment of whether this data suggests a presidential mandate or not. Also, you can look back at your answer to step two in exercise seven, where you predicted overall House seat turnover using a "House Predictor" tool. How close were your predictions to the actual House results?*

19. Another important aspect of judging whether an election delivered a mandate from the voters is to determine whether important new voter groups emerged to influence the election. For example, if lower-income voters voted far more heavily than usual, and overwhelmingly voted for the winning candidate, it could be said that these voters were delivering a mandate for new policies that would benefit them.

20. In the final steps of the previous exercise (exercise ten), you used poll data to examine voter sentiment in this election. Return to your findings from exercise ten, and think again about what you learned about voter groups and their opinions in the 2008 election. *Based on those findings, do you feel that there was an important voter group that meant to deliver a clear message (a "mandate") to the winner of the 2008 election? Explain your answer on the worksheet.*

21. For an election to be called a mandate, there should also be clear policy signals from voters. Politicians must be able to tell the message voters were sending, and what policies they want adopted. To determine whether there were any clear policy messages in the election, one strategy is to review opinion polls. Go to **www.pollingreport.com**.

22. You can see a list of polls in a variety of categories, including a "national priorities" poll under the State of the Union Category, and many other relevant polls in the "In the News" and "Issues" categories. Explore a few of these polls, and determine if you can detect a clear mood of the voters in favor of presidential leadership on an issue. *Based on what you find, summarize on the worksheet whether you think there is a clear issue mandate following this election, or not.*

23. Finally, a key part of any presidential mandate is the general perception among the public, the politicians and the pundits that the mandate exists. If people *think* the President has a mandate, they will generally support his or her leadership and policies, whether or not the voters truly meant to support those ideas in the election. Your final task, therefore, is to examine the "conventional wisdom" around whether the winner of the 2008 election received a popular mandate.

24. To broaden your sense of what the community in general is saying about the idea of a presidential mandate, conduct a Google search of the terms such as: *election, 2008, mandate.* You can also add the name name of the election winner to this list. A long list of links will appear.

25. Browse through some of these links, to see if you can detect a general mood of people celebrating and proclaiming the presidential mandate, or vigorously denying that it exists. Pick one or two interesting links to follow and read or view a bit of what you find on this subject.

26. *On the worksheet, summarize what you have discovered through this limited (and unrepresentative) sample of "conventional wisdom" regarding the presidential mandate. Does the conventional wisdom hold that the president received a mandate or not?*

27. You have examined some of the same data that scholars, politicians, journalists and pundits look at to determine whether the voters were delivering a mandate in the election: the size of the President's victory, the number of seats the President's party gained in Congress, the voter groups that were important, the policy issues that voters seemed to care about, and the conventional wisdom. *Based on all that data, do you conclude that the President-elect has a mandate for change? Or not? Defend your answer on the worksheet.*

Done!

WAS THERE A MANDATE? WORKSHEET

1. Fill in the missing 2008 election data in the chart below. See steps 10 and 11 for how to calculate the missing data.

	Normal Elections	Mandate Elections	Election 2008
Popular Vote Advantage	5.4%	16.6%	
Percent of Electoral Votes	66%	94%	

2. Based on this data, was 2008 a "mandate" election?

3. Fill in the missing 2008 election data in the chart below.

	Normal Elections	Mandate Elections	Election 2008
Seats Gained in the House of Reps. by President's Party	8	39	

4. Based on this data, was 2008 a "mandate" election?

5. Was there a key voter group that emerged in 2008 to deliver a mandate? Defend your answer.

6. Did the voters in 2008 send a clear policy message that could be considered a presidential mandate? Defend your answer.

7. What did you learn about "conventional wisdom" regarding the possibility of a 2008 presidential mandate in your Internet search?

8. Considering all the data you found in this exercise, do you conclude that the 2008 President-elect has a mandate? Defend your answer.

Some people argue that there are "Two Americas." According to this "Two Americas" argument, about half of America lives in "red states" that voted for George W. Bush in the last two elections. These red-state Americans attend church regularly, tend to own guns, don't think much of unions or the United Nations, are strongly opposed to gay marriage and are mostly married and mostly white. The other half of America, living in "blue states" that voted for Gore or Kerry in the last two elections, tend to see the world very differently. "Blue Americans" are more likely to live in a big city, and less likely to own guns or attend church. They are younger than average, tolerant of gay marriage, more racially diverse, and less likely to be married.[1] One British scholar goes so far as to say these blue-state Americans are "a quite European shade of pink."[2]

The "Two Americas" argument draws strength from electoral college maps in the last several presidential elections—maps that seem to show a divided America, with the heavily populated Northeast and West Coast states swinging Democrat and the more rural, Southern and "heartland" states going Republican. Other observers explore different data and different election maps and come up with different conclusions. They note that most states are actually very closely divided between Democrats and Republicans, and that it is more accurate to call them blended "purple" states, rather than "blue" or "red" states. America is not divided between "blue states" and "red states" with different cultures, that is, but is more like a single, closely divided country, purple from coast to coast.

Others look at county-by-county election results and see that Republicans in recent years have won the presidential vote in the vast majority of counties, and that Democrats only compete by piling up huge majorities in a few huge cities like New York, Chicago and Los Angeles. The heart of America and the soul of its common folk are Republican, such observers say, while the Democrats are isolated in a few, mostly coastal, mega-cities. Here's how a *USA Today* journalist described the 2000 election results:

> "Vast stretches of red across the rural heartland, all Republican George W. Bush country. A coastal perimeter and urban patches of blue, where Democrat Al Gore prevailed. ...The two major parties continue to live up to their stereotypical, polarized images: Democrats as a home for women, minorities, gays, immigrants and city dwellers; Republicans as the favorite for men, religious and rural Americans, gun owners and moralists... Can Democrats survive as a bicoastal urban party? Can Republicans survive without making inroads into major population centers?"[3]

What do the results of the 2008 election teach about this notion of a divided, "blue versus red" America (with different regions of the country standing for fundamentally different values), as opposed to notions of a "purple America," with similar and closely divided states, coast to coast? Do the 2008 results suggest that the Electoral College patterns of recent elections continue to endure, or are changes emerging? What are the battleground regions and who won them in 2008? Are the Democrats making inroads into the Rocky Mountains or Deep South? Are the Republicans reaching into America's large population centers? In this exercise, you will explore the answers to such questions.

---

[1] Zogby International. "America Culturally Divided: Blue versus Red States, Democrats versus Republicans—Two Separate Nations," (January 6, 2004), http://zogby.com/news/ReadNews.dbm?ID=775 (accessed on November 6, 2007).
[2] Quoted by Andrew Kohut and Bruce Stokes. "Two Americas, One American." *The Pew Research Center* (June 6, 2006), http://pewresearch.org/pubs/29/two-americas-one-american (accessed on November 6, 2007).
[3] Jill Lawrence. "Map Tells Election Story," *USA Today* (November 11, 2000), http://www.usatoday.com/news/vote2000/pres84.htm (accessed on November 6, 2007).

ELECTORAL GEOGRAPHY:
RED, BLUE OR PURPLE AMERICA?

1. By now, you may have already seen many maps showing how the states voted in 2008. If you have not, or to refresh your memory of America's 2008 electoral breakdown, go to **www.270towin.com**. If the map on the front page does not already display the 2008 election breakdown, select the 2008 election from the menu to the right.

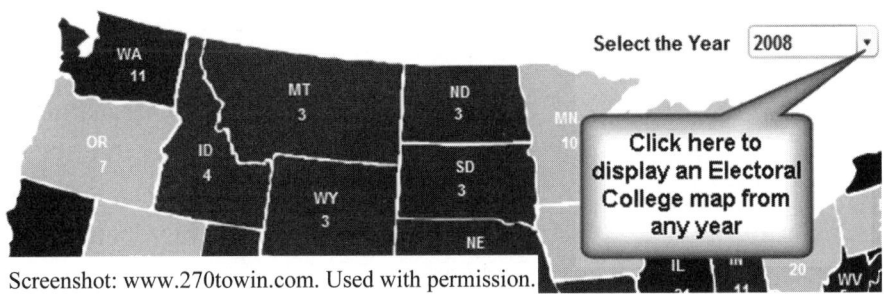

Screenshot: www.270towin.com. Used with permission.

2. Now that you have the map of the actual 2008 election results, you can compare these results to the Electoral College predictions that you came up with earlier, in exercises five and six. In those exercises, you produced maps and predictions of how the election was likely to break down. Look over your predictions, and see how good they were. Based on the outcome, you may pat yourself on the back for your brilliance or scratch your chin in puzzlement. Either way, you'll join a long list of scholarly hits and misses in predicting election results.

3. To better understand whether the 2008 election results reflect enduring trends in America, or suggest shifting loyalties in the states, you need to compare the 2008 results to earlier Electoral College trends.

4. Return to **www.270towin.com**. You can use the "Select the Year" menu box on the right side of the page to view the Electoral College breakdown for any given year. For this exercise pull up the following

election year maps and examine the results (remember, states won by the Democrats are blue and Republican states are red):

- 1988: The Republicans win most of the country, but where do the Democrats maintain some strength?

- 1992 and 1996: The Democrats win these elections. How is the country dividing, in terms of regions that vote Democratic and regions that vote Republican?

- 2000 and 2004: The Republicans win these elections. Are the patterns from the 1990s repeated or do they change?

Based on what you learn in these maps, use your worksheet to summarize which party in the last several elections has been dominant in each of the following five regions of the country (if neither party has been dominant, and the region is a battleground/swing region, note that): the Northeast (1), the Midwest (2), the South (3), the Rocky Mountain West (4), and the Pacific Coast (5). The map below shows which states fall into which regions.

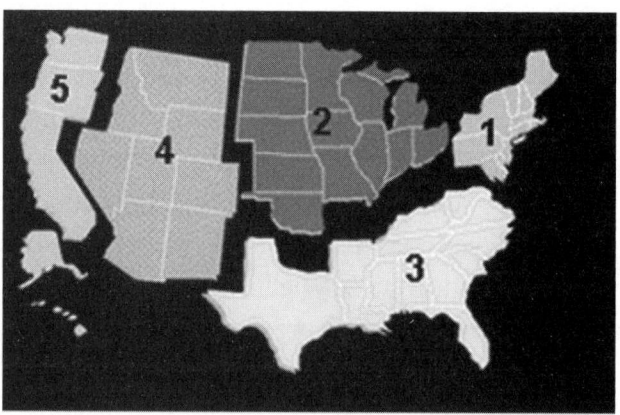

5. Compare these historic trends to the results of the 2008 election. Do the same trends endure, or did one of the parties make progress in a region that has recently been "solid" for the other party? If you

defined a battleground region in step 4, which party, if either, won that battleground region in 2008? *Fill in the answers on your worksheet.*

6. What accounts for the electoral patterns you noticed in step 5? For some analysis of this question, go to **www.cnn.com/POLITICS**. Click the link to "Election Center 2008" near the top of the page (or just scroll down the page to the "Election Center" section).

Screenshot: www.cnn.com

7. Links to numerous articles appear. There is also a button at the top of the page called "**States to Watch**" which you can click for analysis of why various states and regions voted the way they did.

Screenshot: www.cnn.com

8. Spend some time reading the news you find here, until you can summarize at least one key reason why a particular state or region of the country voted as it did. *Summarize that reason on your worksheet.*

9. Electoral maps also help us to draw conclusions about how the country is divided (red states versus blue states), how widespread support for the winning candidate actually was, the nature of rural versus urban voting patterns, and all sorts of similar questions. To explore the ways in which maps electoral maps reveal patterns, and shape how people see their country, go to **www-personal.umich.edu/~mejn/election/**.

10. You are taken to a page that probably has maps posted of the 2008 election. You will look at these in a bit, but first, this page should also have **a link to 2004 presidential election maps.** Click on that link, if the 2004 maps aren't posted on the homepage. There are also links to the 2006 Congressional election maps and other maps on this website, if you want to explore them.

11. When you get to the 2004 presidential election maps, scroll through them and think about how each one suggests a different way of looking at the election.

12. Especially look at the following 2004 election maps and think about how each one reveals a different picture of America:

    - The *"election results by state"* map (the very first one) ("red vs. blue America," suggesting deep divides between the states and a culturally divided America)

    - The first map under the *"election results by county"* section (a "red America" map, suggesting broad-based support for Bush across the country)

    - The third map under the *"election results by county"* section (a "purple America" map, suggesting states are not heavily Democrat nor Republican, but are evenly divided). Also go to **www.princeton.edu/~rvdb/JAVA/election2004** to view additional intriguing "purple America" maps, with descriptive text. This page includes three dimensional maps, which let you view where most voters live, in addition to how they voted.

13. Choose one of these 2004 maps that teaches you something interesting about America. *Summarize what you learned on the worksheet.*

14. Now you can compare the historic maps you have studied to maps of the 2008 election. If you aren't already there, return to **www-personal.umich.edu/~mejn/election/**. Maps of the 2008 presidential election should be posted.

15. Another good source for a 2008 map is **www.uselectionatlas.org**.

16. Finally, for a variety of timely links to interesting 2008 election maps, go to **www.pearson.com/mypolitics**. Click the button for this exercise, and you will find updated links to election maps there.

17. After exploring the maps you find in steps 14 through 16, you should find some interesting maps that reveal facts differently from the traditional "red state versus blue state" Electoral College map that is so common after elections, and which looks something like the map below, from the 2004 election.

18. Using the tools in steps 14-16, find **two** unique maps of the 2008 election that reveal election dynamics differently from the traditional "red state vs. blue state" map. For example, you might find a map of who won the election, county by county (instead of state by state). Or you might discover a three-dimensional map that shows which candidate won certain areas, but also scales those areas for population

size. Or perhaps you can find a map that shows what America would look like, in terms of the state-by-state breakdown of the vote, if only young people voted.

19. *Once you find those two maps, print them and attach them to your worksheet before you hand it in (make sure your map has a clear description/legend attached to it, even if you have to type up the description yourself). Also, on your worksheet, describe why you find each map so interesting.*

Done!

ELECTORAL GEOGRAPHY WORKSHEET

1. Which party, since the 1988 presidential election, has tended to dominate each of these different regions? If neither party has consistently dominated the region, label it a "Battleground."

Northeast	
Midwest	
South	
Rocky Mountain West	
Pacific Coast	

2. Did any of the regions in the list above change their voting habits in 2008? Which party, if either, won the Battleground(s)?

3. Pick one region of the country and analyze why it voted as it did.

4. Summarize the lesson you learned from the 2004 map you selected.

5. Summarize the lessons from two separate maps of the 2008 election (be sure to print those maps to turn in with this assignment).

"You're either on the outside or the inside, and the only thing that can get you on the inside is money." That's how former U.S. Representative Joe Scarborough described the importance of fundraising for anyone running for public office.[1] Former Speaker of the California General Assembly, Jesse Unruh, similarly claims "Money is the mother's milk of politics."

It takes a lot of money to compete in a presidential election. The 2004 elections were the most expensive in history, with George W. Bush and John Kerry each spending about half a billion dollars on their campaigns. Add in independent expenditures by interest groups seeking to influence the election, and total 2004 election costs rise to about $4 billion dollars.[2] The 2008 election looks to shatter these records.

Assuming that substantial contributions relate to who has access to a candidate's ear, it is important to know who is giving all this money, and which interests give the most to which candidates. Are most donors average Americans, with millions of people giving small donations? Or does most of the money come in large donations from affluent big-hitters, large corporations and big unions? Is it true that different social groups support Democrats (unions, lawyers and Hollywood moguls) versus Republicans (the oil and gas lobby and the credit card companies)?

These questions can be answered because election law requires candidates to report the names and group affiliation of their donors, and the amount that each donor gives. The law also requires independent groups (such as the Sierra Club or the Club for Growth) to report the amount they spend to influence elections.

Federal election rules dating back to the 1970s and culminating recently in the 2002 Bipartisan Campaign Reform Act have sought to restrict the amount that any individual or group can give to political campaigns (in an effort to stem corruption and to limit the ability of wealthy social interests to "buy" an election). But as laws have regulated the amount of money that can go directly to a candidate, groups have designed new strategies to spend money to influence elections (such as forming "independent organizations," otherwise known as 527s). The Supreme Court, moreover, has sometimes invalidated aspects of campaign finance laws which the court felt violated a person's right of free speech to spend as much money as they wanted advertising this or that idea or candidate (the most famous case establishing this election free speech right is *Buckley v. Valeo*, 1974).

The state of election law may be complicated, but fortunately for students of elections (and interested citizens), all of these donations and expenditures must be publicly reported to the Federal Election Commission. Many independent groups (such as the Center for Responsive Politics) collect this data from the FEC and offer websites that help visitors to make sense of it all.

In this exercise, you will explore 2008 presidential election campaign finance data. You will learn such things as:

- Which of the candidates received more financial support

- The pattern of large versus small donations to both candidates

- The industries and metropolitan areas that support each party

- Who are the most active 527s (independent political action groups) and which party do they tend to support?

By the end, you will come to a better understanding of who finances presidential races and what that might mean.

---

[1] Quoted in Larry Makinson. *Speaking Freely: Washington Insiders Talk About Money in Politics.* (Washington, D.C.: Center for Responsive Politics, 2003).
[2] For 2004 campaign finance data, see the Center for Responsive politics at www.opensecrets.org/presidential/index_2004.asp (accessed on November 20, 2007).

INVESTIGATING CAMPAIGN FINANCES

1. Go to the Center for Responsive Politics at **www.opensecrets.org**. This is just one of many websites that you can visit to explore campaign finance data. Spend a few minutes exploring the page. Click on different tabs, such as "Who Gives" or "Election Overview," to see what kind of information you can find.

2. When you are done, return to the homepage at **www.opensecrets.org**.

3. For a summary of important aspects of the "Bipartisan Campaign Reform Act" of 2002 (the law which regulates campaign giving), click **"The Basics"** tab at the top of the page, and then choose **"Campaign Finance Law"** from the dropdown menu. A chart appears explaining the basics regulations limiting overall election donations.

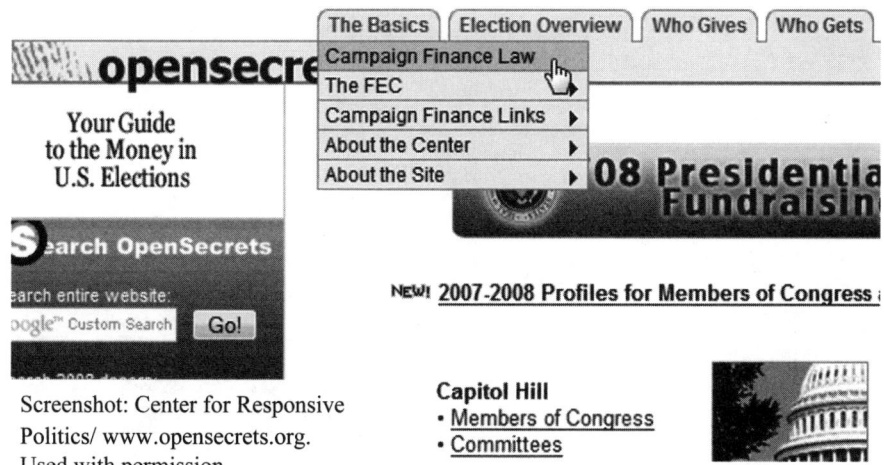

Screenshot: Center for Responsive Politics/ www.opensecrets.org. Used with permission.

4. When you are done examining the chart, you can investigate how the two major presidential candidates did in their fundraising, and what kinds of organizations gave to each candidate. To begin, return to the homepage at **www.opensecrets.org** and click the large button for tracking **2008 Presidential fundraising** (see screenshot on next page).

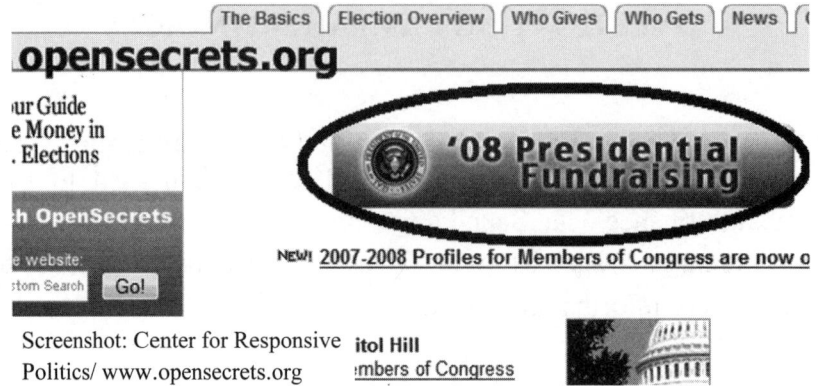

Screenshot: Center for Responsive Politics/ www.opensecrets.org

5. You can now see which of the two major Presidential candidates attracted more financial support. Does the answer surprise you?

6. To gain further details, such as which industries and donors gave to which candidates, **click on the Democratic nominee for president.**

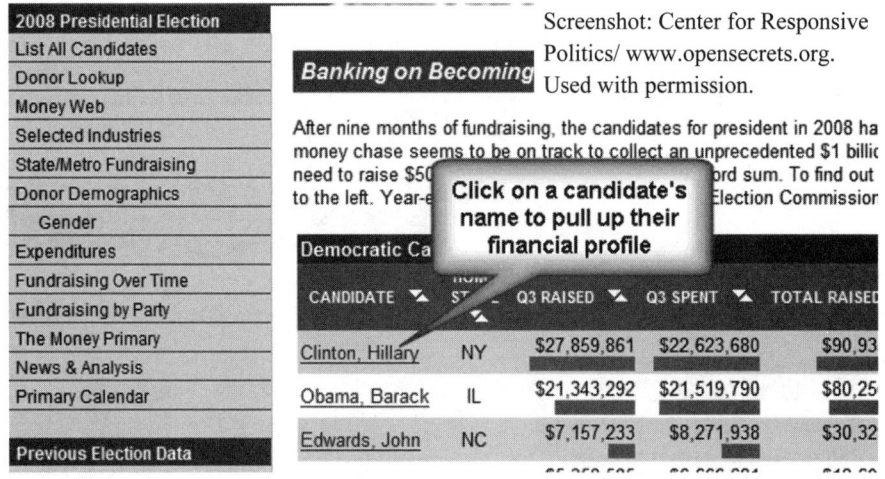

Screenshot: Center for Responsive Politics/ www.opensecrets.org. Used with permission.

7. When the candidate's profile appears, you will see a summary of the candidate's financial position. You can learn more by exploring the menu of tools to the left of the page, under **"2008 Campaign Profile."**

8. Under the **"2008 Campaign Profile,"** go to the **"Geographic Totals"** button to learn the top five metropolitan areas and top four zip codes contributing to the Democratic nominee. *Fill in the worksheet.*

9. Now use the tool for **"Top Industries"** to learn the top four industries contributing to the Democratic nominee. *Fill in the worksheet.*

10. Now use the tool for **"Top Contributors"** to learn the top four group contributors to the Democratic nominee. *Fill in the worksheet.*

11. Repeat steps 8–10 for the Republican nominee. *Fill in the worksheet.*

12. The menu on the left of your screen includes a set of tools under the **"2008 Presidential Election"** label that you can use to further explore presidential fundraising. You can explore which industries give the most to which parties, which states are giving the most to which party, week-by-week fundraising comparisons and much more. Steps 13–18 will use some of the tools in the screenshot on the next page.

2008 Presidential Election
List All Candidates
Donor Lookup
Money Web
Selected Industries
State/Metro Fundraising
Donor Demographics
Gender
Expenditures
Fundraising Over Time
Fundraising by Party
The Money Primary

Screenshot: Center for Responsive
Politics/ www.opensecrets.org.
Used with permission.

13. Begin by clicking the **Money Web** tool. To use the tool, click the bubbles that appear with the names of candidates and various donors.

14. Now examine the kinds of industries giving to each candidate. Click the **"Selected Industries"** option in the menu to the left of the presidential election page. In the **"Display"** menu that appears, you can choose an industry group to examine (for example, you can examine who the oil/gas industry gives to, or who the entertainment industry gives to). *Use this tool to determine any two industry groups that gave more to the Democratic candidate, and any two that gave more to the Republican. Fill in your answers on the worksheet.*

15. Now explore the **"Donor Demographics"** tool in the menu to the left page. Click the **Donor Demographics** link and use the drop down box that appears to sort by **"Percent from Donors of $200 or less."** Your screen will look something like the one on the next page.

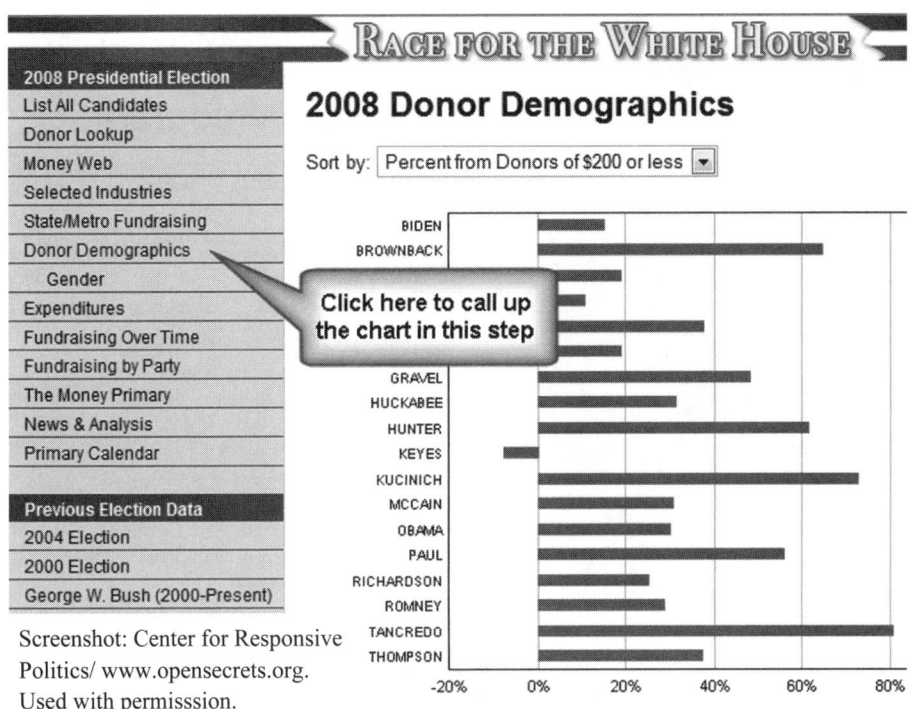

Screenshot: Center for Responsive
Politics/ www.opensecrets.org.
Used with permisssion.

16. Based on this data, which of the two major candidates received more of their support from smaller donors?

17. Repeat this process, but now sort by **"Percent by Donors of $4,600."** Election law states that an individual can only give $2,300 per candidate, per election. But primary and general elections count as two elections, so each individual can give a total of $4,600 directly to a presidential candidate in 2008. *Based on this data, you can determine which party's candidate relied more on big money donors. Was it the Democrats or the Republicans, or was there no real difference? Are you surprised? Why or why not? Fill in the worksheet.*

18. Now explore how the residents of various states tended to donate to one or the other party. Click the link for **"Fundraising by Party"** (in the menu to the left; see screenshot) and explore the map that appears. *What do you learn about the geographic pattern of donations to the two major parties? Provide your answer on the worksheet.*

Screenshot: Center for Responsive
Politics/ www.opensecrets.org.
Used with permission.

19. Finally, you will explore the donations of leading "527" organizations
in the last two presidential elections. Campaign finance law regulates
how much individuals or groups can give directly to candidates or
party committees, but regulations are less strict for "independent"
organizations. There are many organizations that are established to
influence politics (e.g., the Club for Growth, which advocates free-
market policies, or the Sierra Club, an environmentalist group).
Because these groups do not coordinate their activities with specific
candidates, they are classified as "independent" organizations (they are
called 527s after the section of the tax code that they fall under). They
are free to spend as much money as they choose to influence elections,
due to their First Amendment free speech rights. As campaign finance
laws seek to regulate and restrict money going directly to candidates,
an increasing amount of election money is being contributed to and
spent by these 527s. Who are these groups and did they support
Democrats or Republicans more in 2004 and 2008?

20. Click the "**527s**" link on the top of the webpage (see screenshot on
next page).

Screenshot: Center for Responsive Politics/ www.opensecrets.org. Used with permission.

21. When the 527s page appears, choose the **"2004 election cycle"** and choose to view by the **"Top 50 Committees"** (see screenshot).

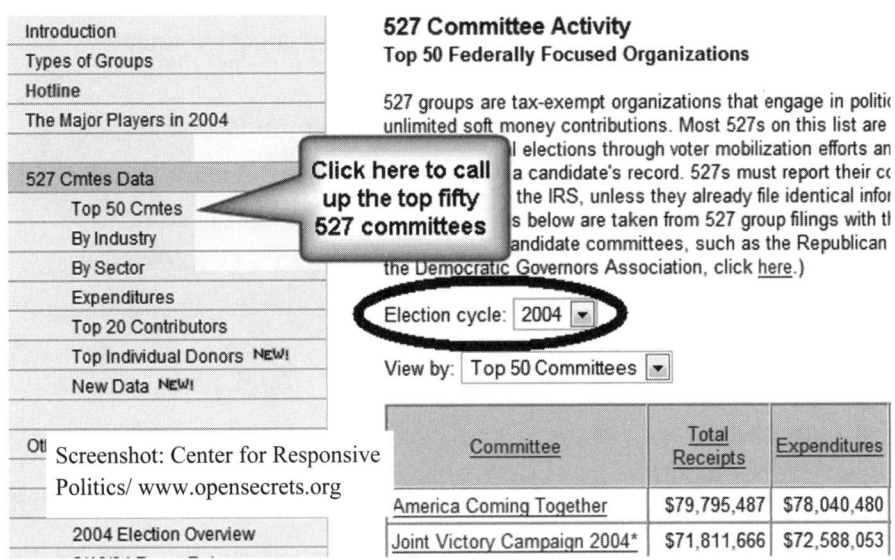

Screenshot: Center for Responsive Politics/ www.opensecrets.org

22. From the list of fifty leading 527s, you can come up with a list of 527 groups which received or spent at least $5 million dollars on the 2004 elections. The list has 16 organizations (the 16 biggest groups in 2004), ending with the International Brotherhood of Electrical Workers.

23. Do most of these groups lean Democrat or Republican? *On the worksheet, place each of the top 16 organizations in the column it belongs (include the amount given by each group).* You can click on the **"2004 Major Player Profile"** link for the organizations to learn more about what party they support (see screenshot on next page).

View by: | Top 50 Committees | ▾ |

Committee	Total Receipts	Expenditures	Federal PAC	2004 Major Player Profile
America Coming Together	$79,795,487	$78,040,480	X	X
Joint Victory Campaign 2004*	$71,811,666	$72,588,053		
Media Fund	$59,414,183	$57,694,580		X
Screenshot: Center for Responsive Politics/ www.opensecrets.org. Used with permission.	18,385,367	$47,695,646	X	X

24. There are four organizations that don't have a profile added to this chart. Here is some information to help you categorize them:

- *Joint Victory Campaign, 2004*: A Dem fundraising group
- *College Republican National Committee*: Republican
- *Citizens for a Strong Senate*: A Pro-Democrat group
- *EMILY'S List*: A group supporting female Democrats
- *Internatl Brotherhood of Electrical Workers*: Pro-Dem union

25. *In the final row of the worksheet, add up total expenditures of each group in the Democratic and Republican columns.* In 2004, which party benefited most from large expenditures by 527s?

26. Now repeat step 23, above, but this time explore the 527 data from the 2008 election cycle. The menu to the left lets you explore the data by the largest 527s, by sector, by industry, and more. *When have finished, use the worksheet to reflect on what you have learned about the role of 527s in the 2008 election. Also reflect on what you think is the most important lesson that you take from this campaign finance exercise.*

Done!

CAMPAIGN FINANCES WORKSHEET

2008	Democratic Nominee	Republican Nominee
Top Four Metro Areas Giving to Candidate		
Top Four Zip Codes Giving to Candidate (include city name)		
Top Four Industries Giving to Candidate		
Top Four Group Contributors to Candidate		

Two Selected Industries that gave more to Democrats than Republicans		
Two Selected Industries that gave more to Republicans than Democrats		

1. Did the Republican or Democratic nominee rely more on big money donors as a percent of all donations they received? Or were the candidates equal? Does the answer surprise you? Why?

2. What did you learn about the geographic pattern of campaign donations to the two major parties?

Leading Democratic 527s in 2004 (Include Dollar Amount Spent)	Leading Republican 527s in 2004 (Include Dollar Amount Spent)
TOTAL Dollars Spent for Dems:	**TOTAL Dollars Spent for Reps:**

3. What did you learn that you find interesting about the pattern of 527 expenditures in the 2008 election?

4. What is the most important lesson that you take from this exercise?

In exercise ten, you investigated important voter groups in recent elections and predicted which voter group might be remembered as the critical group of 2008. In this exercise, you will revisit your earlier prediction, compare it to the actual numbers, and make new assessments about which voter groups were truly the most important and/or surprising in this election, and about what message the voters were trying to send.

It is important to know how different groups are voting, because it reveals something about the state of America, about which groups are organizing to influence politics, and about which kinds of people are standing together or breaking apart in their values. Are conservative Christians standing together to support "family values" Republican candidates? Are Latino and Black voters, who have traditionally voted heavily for Democrats, beginning to consider the GOP as an alternative? Are the Democrats growing their significant advantage among women voters?

Sometimes the answers to these questions reveal the importance of certain groups in influencing the election. In 2004, for example, we learned that church-attending voters, concerned with the "moral standards" of the country, were a powerful force; many credit this group with winning George W. Bush the presidency. In 2006, a significant turnout of black voters, who voted 80-90% for Democrats, proved critical in swinging three Senate seats to the Democratic Party (Virginia, Missouri, and Rhode Island), thus insuring the Democrats gained a majority in the Senate.[1]

Other times, voter behavior suggests important changes emerging in the American public. In 2004, for example, President Bush grew his vote totals among almost every segment of the electorate compared to 2000—nevertheless, Bush *lost* ground among small-town voters, while picking up thousands of new votes in the large cities. Why did the small-town heartland peel away a bit from the Republican Party?[2] Some other unique results emerged in the 2006 elections. A majority of Florida Latinos for the first time voted for Democrats—thus suggesting that the anti-communist, pro-Republican Cuban community in Florida is losing some of its traditional influence. Also, evangelical voters swung away from the Republicans, compared to recent history, suggesting that the "family values" issues were not leading voters to the GOP in the usual way.[3]

Beyond knowing *who* is voting for which candidates, is also important to know *what* message voters were trying to send with their vote, if any. What was on their mind as they selected their next President? In 2006, for example, it is important to know that young voters (aged 18-24) turned out once again in record numbers (beating their 2004 high-water mark). But it is perhaps even more important to know that the top issue on their minds, by far, was opposition to the Iraq War—which led them to vote for Democrats over Republicans by a 60% to 40% margin.[4]

In 2008, who voted and for what? In the following exercise, you will examine exit polls from previous elections, to gain context for understanding results in this election. Then you will study some of the exit polling data from 2008 to determine which groups were critical in this election, and what they were saying with their vote. You will also determine whether your prediction in exercise ten held true or not.

---

[1] "Who Voted and Why," *Democracy Now* (November 10, 2006), www.democracynow.org/article.pl?sid=06/11/10/1426225 (accessed on Nov. 6, 2007).
[2] 2004 Exit Poll data available at www.cnn.com/ELECTION/2004/pages/results/states/US/P/00/epolls.0.html (accessed on Nov. 6, 2007).
[3] Ibid.
[4] "Who Voted and Why," op. cit.

WHO VOTED? FOR WHAT?

1. The best source of information on the demographics of who voted and what they were concerned about are national exit polls. You have already looked at exit poll data in previous exercises, and you will revisit a bit of it here. Begin your exploration of exit polling data by visiting the website of the leading exit polling company: Edison Media Research and Mitofsky International. This group will conduct 2008 exit polling for the Presidential, Senatorial and Gubernatorial races in all 50 states, on behalf of the National Election Pool, which is a consortium of news agencies consisting of ABC, CBS, CNN, FOX, NBC and the Associated Press. These exit polls will interview more than 100,000 voters at 1,000 separate locations nationwide.

2. Go to **www.exit-poll.net**.

3. You are now at the exit poll page of Edison Media Research and Mitofsky International. You can read a general overview of the kind of polling this group completed for the 2008 general election.

4. Unfortunately, comprehensive exit-polling data isn't freely available until some time after the election. Different news agencies (like NBC, or CNN), internet journalists, and some academic institutions pay for access to this information. Without a paid subscription to the raw data, casual researchers like yourself must rely mostly on what's being reported in the news about what the data reveals.

5. In later steps, you will explore some of that current reporting on the exit polls. But first, you can establish some context as to what you are looking for in the 2008 exit poll data by examining exit polls from previous elections.

6. At the bottom of the **www.exit-poll.net** webpage are links to data from previous elections. Begin by examining some data from the last presidential election in 2004. CNN news maintains a good archive (which you have used in previous exercises), so click on the **"CNN"** link under the 2004 election heading.

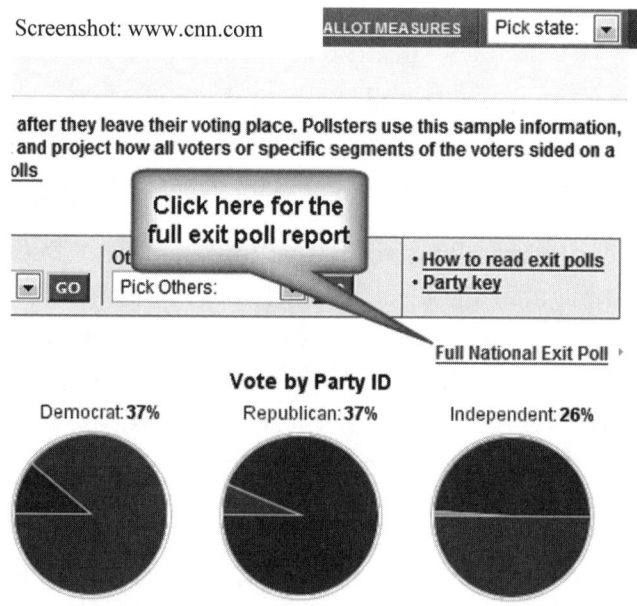

Screenshot: www.exit-poll.net.
Used with permission.

7. You are taken to CNN's 2004 exit poll page. You can see pie charts with data about 2004 election results. Click on the "**Full National Exit Poll**" link, just above the pie charts, as in the screenshot below.

8. You are taken to a long list of different voter categories. In this list you can see all manner of things, such as what percent of voters were males, what percent were black, what percent went to church regularly, what percent cared mostly about "moral values," etc.

9. The screenshot below shows you how the exit poll data is presented, and gives you tips on how to read the exit polls. As described in the screenshot, you can see that 54% of all voters in 2004 were females,

and 48% of these female voters voted for Bush. The data in the light grey "2000" column shows that Bush gained 5% more of the female vote in 2004 than in 2000.

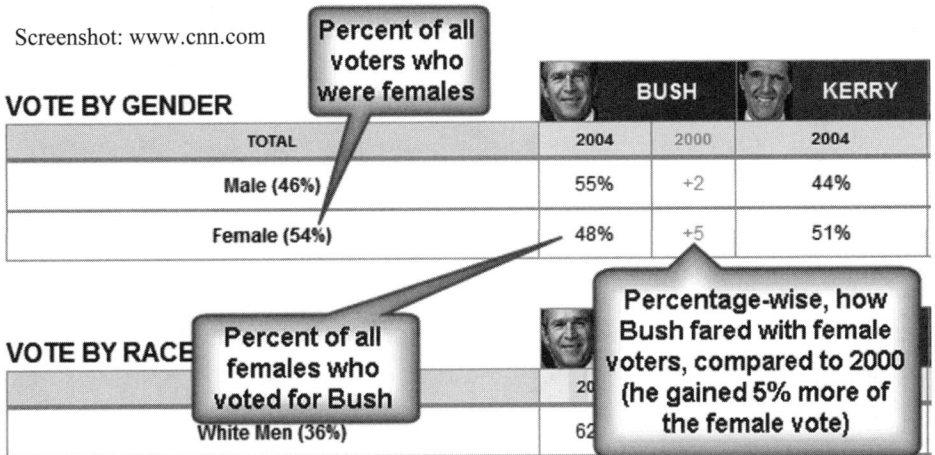

10. Spend some time scrolling through this list of polling questions asked after the 2004 presidential election. Based on your review, come up with three categories of data that reveal interesting patterns in the 2004 election. For example, you might choose the charts that reveal how voters broke down based on their age, their church attendance practices, and their concerns about health care.

11. *List the three voter categories you examined and summarize their voting behavior in the spreadsheet provided at the end of this exercise. That spreadsheet includes rows for you to input this data; they are titled "2004 Category 1," "2004 Category 2," and "2004 Category 3." Fill in the three voter categories with the names of your chosen voter groups (e.g., "white men," or "active church-goers"), and report on their voting patterns in 2004. An example of how "Northeasterners" voted is provided in the spreadsheet, to help you in filling out this data.*

12. Now return to **www.exit-poll.net**.

13. This time, click on the CNN exit polling data for the **2006** congressional elections—**be careful to select the 2006 exit poll, NOT the 2004 exit poll link.**

Check out our Consumer Exit Polling section for more info various projects that Edison Media Research has worked

Click here

Vi w 2006 **Exit Poll Results** on our member web sites at:

CNN, **CBS**, **NBC**, **FOX**

Screenshot: www.exit-poll.net.
Used with permission.

14. You are taken to an archive of exit poll data from the 2006 congressional elections. This data is important to understanding changes or enduring patterns in voter sentiment in 2008, since it is more recent than data from 2004. Even though there was no national level election in 2006 (all congressional elections were state-level), the exit polling data reveals national patterns by adding up voter poll results from all congressional races across the nation and reporting them in a single 2006 "national exit poll." The chart you see on this page consolidates the data from *all* races for the U.S. House of Representatives and reports it as a single national exit poll.

15. Review the data you find on this webpage. It is likely that some or all of the categories of data you choose to focus on in step 10, above, are also included in this 2006 election poll. Compare the 2004 voter categories that you looked at to those same voter categories in the 2006 results. You can do this by comparing Bush's percent of the vote in 2004 to the Republican percent of the vote in 2006, and comparing Kerry's percent of the vote in 2004 to the Democratic percent of the vote in 2006.

For example, in the screenshots on the next page, you can see that Kerry (the Democrat) received only 37% of the white male vote in 2004, but Democrats as a whole received 44% of the white male vote in the 2006 congressional elections. This might suggest growing Democratic strength among white male voters.

Screenshot: www.cnn.com

VOTE BY RACE AND GENDER	BUSH		KERRY
TOTAL	2004	2000	2004
White Men (36%)	62%	n/a	37%
White Women (41%)	55%	n/a	44%

VOTE BY RACE AND GENDER (2006 Congressional Elections)

TOTAL	Democrat	Republican
White Men (39%)	44%	53%
White Women (40%)	49%	50%
Non-White Men (9%)	75%	23%

16. Compare the 2004 and 2006 results for the three categories you chose to focus on in step 10. If one or more of your categories from 2004 aren't repeated in the 2006 data, just focus on the categories that are repeated. *Report your findings on the spreadsheet at the end of this exercise.* You can begin to note whether voter patterns seem to be enduring or changing in these categories, between 2004 and 2006. You will reflect on those patterns in a later step in this exercise.

17. Now select two categories of data that are *different* than those you selected in step 10. *On the spreadsheet, list the two new categories you selected (i.e., fill in the voter category names under "2006 Category 1" and "2006 Category 2"). Include data about the percent of voters voting Democrat or Republican in these categories in 2006.*

18. Now you know some important details about how voters behaved in 2004 and 2006, and how that behavior was related to such things as voter income, voter race, the size of the voter's city and voter opinion on such things as Iraq, abortion and gay marriage. In the following steps you will compare these findings to 2008 exit polling data.

19. There are many places where you can find reports on voter behavior in the 2008 presidential election. Begin by going to **www.pearson.com/ mypolitics** and clicking on the link to this exercise. Information will

appear guiding you to good sites reporting 2008 exit polling data. In addition, four other good sites to examine for voter polls are:

- **www.cnn.com/ELECTION/2008** (CNN's archive of political reporting on the election)

- **www.foxnews.com/politics/youdecide2008** (FOX news archive on 2008 election reporting)

- **www.washingtonpost.com/wp-dyn/content/politics/** (Washington Post election reporting archive)

- **www.pollingreport.com** (a collection of national polls revealing voter opinion on a variety of timely political issues)

20. You needn't explore every one of these sites, and you should feel free to examine other sites that you might be familiar with. Whatever sites you explore, you need to read articles and examine polls to find details on what was on voters' minds as they voted in this year's elections. You should also browse data about how voters broke down in terms how the different sexes, races, income levels, and age levels voted, etc.

21. As a final supplement, you could explore the collection of polls and analysis found at Rasmussen Reports website—one of America's most respected polling companies. Go to **www.rasmussenreports.com**. Once there, click on the "politics" link in the main menu to the left of the page, and you will find a collection of recent polls and related political analysis. Review any of it that you like in learning about various groups of voters and why they behaved as they did in 2008.

Screenshot: www.rasmussenreports.com. Used with permission.

22. Based on your review of 2008 voter data in the previous steps, come up with five categories of 2008 voter behavior data that you can compare to the five categories of 2004 and 2006 voter behavior data that you reported on previously in this exercise. *On the spreadsheet, summarize how voters in 2008 voted in the five voter categories that you previously reported on for 2004 and 2006.*

    If you simply cannot discover voter data from 2008 to compare to a category of data that you looked at from 2004 or 2006, just leave that category out. What you are interested in determining is if the earlier voter patterns that you identified in 2004 and 2006 stayed the same or changed in 2008.

23. Finally, your review of 2008 voter behavior data probably revealed some interesting patterns that were different from those you reported on for 2004 and 2006. Find at least one issue or demographic pattern that the media and polls reported on for 2008 voter patterns that is different from any of the data you reported on for 2004 and 2006. For example, you might find that in 2008 pollsters spend a lot of time asking voters about how they feel about voting for a female candidate, or how they feel about global warming. Or you might report on how a certain demographic of voters, such as college-educated voters, or voters in the Rocky Mountains, voted in 2008. *On the spreadsheet, list this "new" 2008 issue or voter group and summarize how voters on this issue or from this demographic group behaved (i.e., the percent that voted Democratic or Republican on this issue).*

24. Now your spreadsheet reports on a range of voter data in six different categories, and you have seen a good deal of other data that you didn't include on your spreadsheet. On the basis of all this data, you can now reflect on whether the "key group" predictions that you made in an earlier exercise have held true. *On the worksheet that follows the spreadsheet, share your conclusions about what the 2008 exit polling data reveals in terms of whether your "key voter group" predictions from exercise ten were correct (skip this step if you did not complete exercise ten).*

25. Finally, use the worksheet to share your conclusions about such things as what the exit polling data over the last three elections reveals about whether the voters are shifting their voting patterns over the last four years, or whether they are maintaining the same voting habits. Or you could reflect on what the data suggests in terms of which voters tend to support Democrats versus Republicans. Or you could reflect on what this data from the last three elections tells us about the nature of the American people. Based on all the data you have investigated, what can you now say about American values? *Use the worksheet to reflect on any of these kinds of larger questions that you find meaningful.*

Done!

WHO VOTED? FOR WHAT? WORKSHEET

Voter Category	2004	2006	2008
EXAMPLE: Northeasterners	Rep: 43% Dem: 56%	Rep: 35% Dem: 63%	Fill in this cell with 2008 data
2004 Category 1			
2004 Category 2			
2004 Category 3			
2006 Category 1			
2006 Category 2			
2008 Category			

1. Now that you have reviewed the 2008 exit polling data, what can you say about the accuracy of your key voter group predictions that you produced earlier, in exercise ten?

2. What does the data in this exercise reveal in terms of whether voters are shifting their voting patterns or maintaining the same habits? Alternatively, what does the data suggest in terms of which voters tend to support Democrats and which support Republicans? What else have you learned about American voters?

ISSUE ONE: DEFINING THE DEMOCRATS

1. What do you think of how the Democrats are reaching out to specific voter groups?

2. Is the Democratic nominee an inspiring speaker? Does it matter?

3. Based on what you have learned here (and elsewhere), would you call yourself a Democrat? Why or why not?

ISSUE TWO: DEFINING THE REPUBLICANS

1. What have you learned about differences and similarities in how Democrats and Republicans target unique voter groups?

2. Is the Republican nominee an inspiring speaker? Does it matter?

3. Based on what you have learned here (and elsewhere), would you call yourself a Republican? Why or why not?

ISSUE THREE: PUBLIC OPINION

1. Is it appropriate for candidates to constantly seek out and react to public opinion polling data?

2. If there were no public opinion polls at all, would the current state of politics in general and elections specifically be improved or not?

3. If you were to advise one of the presidential candidates, what would be your key piece of advice in terms of what the candidate most needs to know about public opinion in 2008?

ISSUE FOUR: INVESTIGATING CAMPAIGN ADS

1. Can voters learn important things about candidates or political issues from short 30 second television ads? If there were no television ads, do you think voters would take the initiative to learn about candidates in other ways?

2. Do negative attack ads play an important role in educating voters, or are they mostly useless distractions?

3. Should independent groups be allowed to spend as much as they want on election advertising (as a free speech right), or should there be clear limits on advertising expenditures, by any group?

ISSUE FIVE: THE ELECTORAL COLLEGE BATTLEGROUND

1. Why do you think the Democratic base states vote so reliably for Democrats? What do Republican base states share that make them safe for Republican candidates?

2. What reasons can you come up with to explain why this year's "swing states" aren't clearly lining up behind the Republican or the Democratic candidate?

3. The Electoral College leads candidates to target a limited number of specific states for special attention during the presidential race, as opposed to running a race with national media ads and targeting mainly the largest population centers. Can you think of some reasons why the Electoral College's influence might be bad for a democratic system? In what ways is it good?

ISSUE SIX: TARGETING THE BATTLEGROUND STATES

1. What do you think voters in battleground states most want to hear from presidential candidates: ways in which that candidate will specifically help the voters of that state, or ways in which the candidate will lead the nation in general to a better place? In other words, should a candidate carefully target a variety of local messages to each specific state's voters, or should a candidate consistently offer the same kind of national message?

2. In this exercise, you investigated demographics that are favorable to one of the two major parties. Why do you think voters in those demographics tend to support the party you chose to focus on?

3. What are your thoughts on the fact that voters in battleground states receive far more attention from candidates than voters in other states?

ISSUE SEVEN: PREDICTING THE SWING SEATS

1. Do you think the current presidential candidates will have long coattails or not? Why?

2. Is it generally better for the nation when a president comes into office with a large majority in Congress, or does divided government (different parties in control of Congress and the presidency) serve the nation better?

3. Most incumbents in the Senate and House hold "safe seats" that no challenger can really hope to win. As a strategy to force out such incumbents, would you support term limits? Why or why not?

ISSUE EIGHT: PRESIDENTIAL DEBATES

1. The introduction to this exercise raised the following questions, by Jamieson and Birdsell: "Do [the debates] test knowledge and vision? Do they sort good ideas from bad? Do they reveal important character traits and habits of mind to the voters? In short, do they provide voters with what they need to know to choose a president?" What is your response to those questions?

2. Who "won" this year's presidential debates? Why?

3. Should Third Party candidates regularly be invited to join the debates, in addition to the major candidates? Why or why not?

ISSUE NINE: EVALUATING THE MEDIA

1. Thomas Patterson criticizes the media for interpreting policy initiatives and campaign appearances as strategically chosen in order to manipulate voters and win the election (rather than analyzing how policies might actually help or hurt voters). But are media reports correct in their "games" interpretation? How much do you think candidates are motivated by strategic considerations of building popularity, as compared to being motivated by a commitment to principles and policies to improve their country?

2. Based on what you have seen on television news, would you say TV programs such as Fox News or CNN are more or less likely than newspapers to offer serious policy and leadership coverage?

3. Who do you blame for low voter turnout and rising cynicism? Apathetic voters, dismal politicians, or a distorting media?

ISSUE TEN: KEY VOTER GROUPS

1. Do you think most voters care more about how a candidate will improve the voter's own individual situation, or do voters care more about the good of the country as a whole? In other words, how much time should candidates spend courting individual groups of voters with specific policy ideas targeted to that group (e.g., women, gun-owners, church-goers), and how much time should the candidate spend on presenting a broad and consistent national vision?

2. In recent years, regular church-going voters have voted heavily Republican, while Latinos and Blacks have voted heavily Democratic. What accounts for these kinds of results?

3. What do you think accounts for the "gender gap"—the fact that women vote significantly more Democratic, while men vote more Republican?

ISSUE ELEVEN: WAS THERE A MANDATE?

1. Did the President-elect receive a mandate in 2008?

2. Do you think voters can be educated and united enough on issues to deliver a mandate through an election?

3. Who do you think best represents the will and values of the American people: the Congress (whose members are elected from districts all across the country) or the President (who is elected by voters on a national level)? Why?

ISSUE TWELVE: ELECTORAL GEOGRAPHY

1. What is the most important geographical change (if any) in 2008 voting patterns, as compared to previous elections?

2. Is America really divided between "red" and "blue" states, with different values emerging in different regions? Or is the country generally similar from coast to coast, with national divisions showing up just as much *within* states as they do *between* them?

3. Will America in the future be characterized more by "red state" or "blue state" values? Which direction is the country heading?

ISSUE THIRTEEN: CAMPAIGN FINANCES

1. Why do you think most people give contributions to political candidates? What are they expecting, if anything, in return?

2. Should individuals and organized groups be restricted in how much they can spend to influence an election? Or would such restrictions be a violation of their free speech rights?

3. How do you think politics would change if a taxpayer-supported fund paid most election expenses for candidates for federal office?

ISSUE FOURTEEN: WHO VOTED? FOR WHAT?

1. What message (if any) did voters try to send in election 2008?

2. In what ways have voters changed, in terms of their priorities and voting habits, since 2004?

3. In what ways are voting patterns remaining the same since 2004?